M000036271

Liars & Legends

Emily Ellison & Chuck Perry

Foreword by George Lindsey

RUTLEDGE HILL PRESS

Nashville, Tennessee

A Division of Thomas Nelson Publishers

Since 1798

www.thomasnelson.com

TM, SM and © 2005 Turner Regional Entertainment Network, Inc. A Time Warner Company. All Rights Reserved.

No portion of this book may be reproduced, stored in a retrieval system, or transmitted in any form or by any means—electronic, mechanical, photocopy, recording, or any other—except for brief quotations in printed reviews, without the prior permission of the publisher.

Published by Rutledge Hill Press, a Division of Thomas Nelson, Inc., P.O. Box 141000, Nashville, Tennessee, 37214.

Rutledge Hill Press books may be purchased in bulk for educational, business, fundraising, or sales promotional use. For information, please email SpecialMarkets@ThomasNelson.com.

Library of Congress Cataloging-in-Publication Data

Ellison, Emily.
    Liars & legends / Emily Ellison & Chuck Perry ; foreword by George Lindsay.
      p. cm.
    Includes index.
    ISBN 1-4016-0203-7 (hardcover)
    1. Legends—Southern States. 2. Curiosities and wonders—Southern States. 3. Southern States—History—Anecdotes. 4. Southern States—History, Local—Anecdotes. 5. Southern States—Biography—Anecdotes. I. Title: Liars and legends. II. Perry, Chuck. III. Title.
    F209.6.E44 2005
    975—dc22
                                         2005000135

Printed in the United States of America

05 06 07 08 09—5 4 3 2 1

Contents

Foreword

ANYONE BORN IN THE SOUTH, OR WHO HAS SPENT MUCH TIME HERE, KNOWS that being called a "liar" ain't always bad.

For example, when your aunt discovers that her no-account husband went fishing instead of going to visit a sick buddy as he said he was, she's likely to mutter under her breath, "That lyin' rascal." That's really a term of endearment, and what she really means is that after forty-two years of marriage, she should have known better.

Or suppose two fishing buddies are talking about your ne'er-do-well uncle, and one says to the other, "He'd lie on credit when he could get cash for the truth." What that really means is that your uncle is a great storyteller who is just inclined to put a little rouge and lipstick on some of his tales.

So when Turner South decided to name a television show *Liars & Legends*, and later decided to publish a book with the same title, they didn't mean that some of the stories would be untrue. They were just tipping you off that some kernels of truth in each story might have been puffed up with a little hot air, just to make them tastier.

And as for the "legends" part, well, a legend is just a good story that has been told so many times that it sounds like the gospel truth.

So sit back and enjoy this collection of stories about "liars and legends." And if you read closely enough, maybe you'll be able to tell the difference.

— **George Lindsey**

Introduction

BETWEEN US, WE HAVE LIVED AT ONE TIME OR ANOTHER IN MOST OF THE states that are generally considered the southeastern United States (Alabama, Florida, Georgia, Mississippi, Tennessee, North and South Carolina), and have traveled well the rest of them (Kentucky, Louisiana, Maryland, Virginia, and West Virginia). From Key West, Florida—where at Hemingway's run-down home his beloved six-toed cats seemed to hang from the trees like mangoes and avocados—to the pristine order and symmetry of Jefferson's gardens and rooms at Monticello; from the Great Smoky Mountains to the Natchez Trace; from Kill Devil Hills to Montgomery, we have been privileged to be students of the South.

We have looked over the proverbial gates and fences and sometimes played the courses at Augusta, Southern Pines, Pinehurst, Kiawah, Ponte Vedra, and Highlands. We've eaten at barbecue joints, Walgreen's counters, and drugstore fountains from Wake Forest to Birmingham and taken the overnight Southern Crescent from Brookwood Station to New Orleans.

We've netted floating flounder and crab at one of the miraculous predawn "Jubilees" on Mobile Bay and sailed the same waters on hot summer days at dusk just beyond the Grand Hotel. We've kayaked on southern man-made lakes where new, ten-thousand-square-foot homes dot the shorelines like modernist boulders, and we've rafted Appalachian rivers and streams where hulking rusting skeletons of trucks and automobiles were planted along the water banks to help arrest erosion.

We've caught rainbow trout in Betty's Creek in north Georgia and bounded up the sides of Stone Mountain and the falls at Amicalola. We've galloped across pastures in South Carolina; hiked along narrow, laurel-lined trails in North Carolina; and strolled through the streets of colonial towns in Virginia. And, like most adolescents, we've traveled—grim-faced, belligerent, and open-windowed—in the backseats of our parents' cars to visit relatives and sites from Nags Head to Sarasota.

The land of our birth and rearing is a place where, even with the sophisticated and worldly restaurants of Atlanta and Charleston, Savannah and Charlotte, there are still within shouting distance family kitchens and restaurants that serve vegetables cooked to "sweet collapse," as Rita Mae Brown has written, and where fatback is a staple.

It is a land of great "college towns": Chapel Hill, Charlottesville, Nashville, Williamsburg, Athens, New Orleans, Baton Rouge, Charlotte, Columbia, Winston Salem, Atlanta, and Durham. It is the land of Carolina snowdrifts and Florida Panhandle oysters. It is a land where cotton may no longer be king, but in some places tobacco, air flight, and Yankee tourists are.

Lord help us, this is sometimes still the land of William Faulkner and Tennessee Williams, of Flannery O'Connor and Carson McCullers. It is the territory mined and mined again, often with brilliance and unrelenting perspicuity, by such dissimilar sensibilities as Eudora Welty, Zora Neale Hurston, Robert Penn Warren, Peter Taylor, Anne Tyler, Bobbie Ann Mason, Robb Forman Dew, Reynolds Price, Alice Walker,

Josephine Humphreys, Harper Lee, Pat Conroy, Raymond Andrews, Erskine Caldwell, Alex Haley, Ferrol Sams, Terry Kay, Louis D. Rubin, James Alan McPherson, Lee Smith, Gail Godwin, and a host of others.

This is the land of sleeping-porches and ceiling fans, of sterling tea services and aching poverty, of flagstone walks and boxwood hedges, of proper parlors and musky pool halls, of forever-damp basements and crawlspaces, of slime-covered swimming pools and brain-broiling attics.

This is the region we know best. It remains so much the same since our youth and yet is so irrevocably different. Simultaneously it is unique and homogenized, sorrowful and jubilant, irreverent and pious.

It is a place where our first names (Chu-uk and Em'ly) can be spoken with two syllables.

This is the South, *our* South, for good and for ill. Its landscape has inspired so many banal paintings of buckets and barns, so much prose overflowing with Spanish moss and kudzu, and so many films overpowered with magnolias and fake southern accents that much of what is authentic about the region has devolved into cliché.

But amidst all the stereotypes and platitudes, Turner South's *Liars & Legends* series has proven there are still some originals out there. The producers, writers, editors, and videographers have illuminated some of the unique corners of a still-fascinating place and a multicultured people. They have shown with equal enthusiasm the dizzying mountain roads that bisect the Appalachian Trail and the endless lonesome stretches of southern Georgia, northern Florida, eastern Mississippi, and western Louisiana.

Once a frontier and an agrarian society, the South is becoming a region of malls with Roman-empire sameness, a land intersected with an interstate highway system and discount outlets and fast-food chains. Although the area is larger than the size of Western Europe, in little more than half a day's time you can go from shore to mountain, from international diversity to segregation. It is a place of grand raconteurs who dare not let details get in the way of a good story; a place where there's often a flimsy line between fact and fiction, liar and legend.

It is as dichotomous a region as exists on the planet and as different in every respect as the people who inhabit it. When we've been lucky, we've explored it together. Even on the most familiar ground, we occasionally feel like interlopers and strangers. But at our late great ages, it is the place we still call home.

— Emily Ellison and Chuck Perry
Atlanta, Georgia

Chapter 1

Build It and They Will Come

THE SOUTH IS ONE OF THE MOST DIVERSE REGIONS OF AMERICA. FROM mountains to beaches, farm communities to major cities, barbecue to sushi, Little League to the Major Leagues, you can find almost anything you're looking for . . . and several things you probably never thought to look for.

Take, for example, a castle built from huge blocks of coral by a diminutive, eccentric man; or an old-fashioned western town where cars are prohibited; or the largest collection of kangaroos outside of Australia.

The Coral Castle

Scientists and engineers today marvel at the achievements of builders thousands of years ago—Stonehenge in southern England, the great pyramids of Egypt, and the mysterious statues on Easter Island continue to confound us.

But you don't have to travel the world to find such mysteries. In Homestead,

1

Florida, approximately twenty-five miles southwest of Miami, is an equally inexplicable building achievement—the Coral Castle.

Edward Leedskalnin was born in Riga, Latvia, in 1887, into a family of stonemasons. Edward came to Florida City in 1918. Five years earlier, at age twenty-six, he was engaged to be married to the love of his life, sixteen-year-old Agnes Scuffs, whom he affectionately referred to as "Sweet Sixteen." But the day before their wedding, Agnes cancelled the ceremony. Heartbroken, Edward left Latvia for America. He lived in Canada, California, and Texas before settling in Florida, reportedly for health considerations (he had contracted a mild case of tuberculosis while working in a Canadian lumber camp).

With twelve dollars in savings, Edward purchased an acre of land in then-desolate Florida City, ten miles from Homestead. Within a year, he had begun single-handedly to quarry huge chunks of coral from the land and carve them into different shaped building stones. Barely more than five feet tall and weighing only one hundred pounds, Edward was an unlikely prospect to build such mammoth structures.

Grounds of Coral Castle

The gate to his Rock Gate Park, as it was originally called, weighs nine tons and measures ninety-two inches high, eighty inches wide, and twenty-one inches thick. It pivots through an iron rod sitting atop an automobile gear. The massive door, with only a quarter-inch gap between its frame on all sides, is so perfectly balanced that it opens at the touch of a hand. Inside Edward erected a two-story square tower (his living and working space) from coral blocks weighing four to nine tons each—the entire tower is said to have weighed approximately 243 tons. Huge coral representations of planets, moons, and suns dotted the property; coral rocking chairs, each weighing a ton but moving with the ease of a normal rocker, were placed about the compound.

Perfectly balanced, this door weighs nine tons and can be opened by a child's touch.

Neighbors were naturally curious about this eccentric little man who lived alone. No workers were ever seen on the property, but structures continued to rise from the flat, sandy soil. The secretive Edward worked only at night to avoid prying eyes, and he sustained himself with a small garden, a freshwater well, and small game that he trapped. He occasionally rode a bicycle three and one-half miles to town for other vital provisions. When asked why he was building this unusual place, Edward would only say that it was in homage to his "Sweet Sixteen."

Were astrological symbols a clue to his secret?

But how did this tiny man working alone manage to move such huge blocks of coral? Teenagers spying on him one night said they saw coral blocks "floating through the air like balloons," but no one ever confirmed their story.

By 1936 development was encroaching on Florida City and the reclusive Leedskalnin. He bought ten acres of land in nearby Homestead, Florida, with money saved from doing odd jobs and repairs for area farmers. During the next four years, Edward methodically relocated his Rock Gate Park to the new location. Each piece was placed on a pair of iron girders sitting atop a truck chassis. Every morning a driver showed up with his tractor, hitched up the chassis, and towed it ten miles to Homestead. The driver then unhitched the loaded chassis and took back the empty one from the day before. When he arrived the following morning, another loaded chassis would be ready for moving. No one ever saw the massive coral blocks loaded, unloaded, or put in place.

When the move was finally completed, about 1940, Leedskalnin built an eight-foot-high coral wall around the new site. Each block was approximately four feet wide and three feet thick. All totaled, Edward had quarried, shaped, and moved more than eleven hundred tons (2.2 million pounds) of coral using no powered tools.

More than 2.2 million pounds of coral was used for this Coral Castle.

At the new location, Edward became slightly more social and occasionally allowed visitors to see his creation for twenty-five cents. When asked how he managed to move such huge stones, Leedskalnin would only say, "I have discovered the secrets of the pyramids and have found out how the Egyptians and the ancient builders in Peru, Yucatan, and Asia, with only primitive tools, raised and set in place blocks of stone weighing many tons. If I can figure it out, so can you."

Leedskalnin became ill in December 1951. He took a bus to the hospital in Miami and died there three days later at the age of sixty-four. A nephew living in Michigan inherited Rock Gate Park but sold it in 1953. Shortly afterward the name was changed to the Coral Castle, and it became the popular tourist attraction it remains today.

Entering Coral Castle

Edward never shared his secret with anyone. The only written documents he left were five pamphlets, including three on magnetic currents. He believed that "all matter consists of magnets which can produce measurable phenomena, and electricity." He said that he had "rediscovered the laws of weight, measurement, and leverage," and that those concepts "involved the relationship of the Earth to celestial alignments."

The small Latvian with only a fourth grade formal education apparently discovered a way to reduce Earth's gravitational pull. Yet the pull of his secret is stronger today than ever.

Love Valley

Love Valley, the smallest incorporated town in North Carolina, is located in the mountains north of Statesville and Interstate 40, approximately 132 miles—as the crow flies—from the state capital of Raleigh on the south side of Fox's Mountain. The town was founded in 1954 and incorporated in 1963 by Jetter Andy Barker, who currently is serving his sixteenth term as mayor.

Throughout his childhood Andy Barker loved horses, cowboys, and westerns. He loved the simplicity of that lifestyle, where every town had a blacksmith, a general store, a tack store, and a good place to grab a bite or "wet your whistle." Where horses provided labor and transportation and carriages were not powered by internal combustion engines. Where honor, honesty, and loyalty formed the foundation of the community, and where residents looked after each other. Such an idealistic place would have had an appropriate name like Love Valley.

But rather than sit around pining for that nineteenth-century lifestyle, Andy Barker and his wife, Ellenora, decided to create it right there in northwestern North

The main street in Love Valley is like a scene from another century.

Carolina. They left their successful construction business and comfortable life in Charlotte, bought a tract of land in the Brushy Mountains, and built a working western town with a one-hundred-yards-long dirt main street, authentic looking facades, wooden sidewalks, and hitching posts in front of the stores.

"From the time I was in the fourth or fifth grade, I was gonna build me a western town," said Barker. "I was twenty-eight when I came up here and started the town. Everybody, including my family, thought I'd lost my mind. I've never gotten it back."

The first permanent structure they built, right in the middle of town, was Love Valley Presbyterian Church.

"Building the church and then building the community around it—that's the way to go," Barker said. "We've had nine other western towns built in North Carolina, and they didn't make it. This is the one that stayed. Rest of 'em are gone by the wayside."

No cars are allowed in Love Valley, which boasts a permanent population of ninety-six people but swells on weekends and during special events throughout the year—including Mule Day, an annual chili cook-off, and regular rodeos in a fifty-five-hundred-seat arena. The stores are open Friday through Sunday year-round and cater to thousands of campers and tourists, many of whom bring their horses with them. "All the prices in town are very competitive," said Barker.

Modern-day cowboys hightail-it through the streets.

"This is not a rip-off place. In fact, I tell the storeowners, 'Keep your prices reasonable, or else I'll build competition and put you out of business.'

There are no fake show-downs in Love Valley.

"You see, I wanted a real working western town, not one of those places where people come to see staged shoot-outs and that sort of thing. What's here is real. If you see somebody squaring off to shoot, you'd better run. But we've been lucky up here. We've never had anybody shot," added Barker. "Course, we have had about seven folks shoot their legs while practicing their fast draw."

Like authentic western towns, Love Valley also has a jail. "We've had 556 locked up in there . . . drunkenness, mostly. But they made us close it about ten years ago," explained Barker. "Jail inspector came in and told me if I didn't close it, he'd put me in jail and throw away the key."

Barker pointed out the bars on one of the jail's windows. "We had a couple of cowboys come in with a car one night and pull out those bars to spring their buddies out of jail. I saw the car and said, 'Hey, what are you doing with that car here—they're not allowed.' And one of them said, 'Shhhh. I just broke my buddies out of jail.' So I got their license plate number and let 'em go, but the state police caught 'em between here and Statesville. At that time we had a mayor's court. When they walked into court, one of 'em looked at me and said, 'Oh no!' and I said, 'Oh yes!'"

Buddy Price is one of the permanent residents. He owns and operates Love Valley Stables on weekends and during peak season when renting horses is big business, but most of the time he's a contractor.

"You could easily shut your eyes in Love Valley and pretend it's a hundred years ago," said Price, a lifelong resident of the North Carolina mountains. "There are lots of trails around here—probably more than anywhere

Life seems simpler in a non-motorized setting.

else east of the Mississippi. You can just take off and ride. People around here are all accommodating and friendly, unless you get right up in their front yard."

The most accommodating of all, of course, is eighty-year-old Andy Barker. He's a man who built his dream and invited others to share it.

The Kangaroo Conservation Center

Atlanta, Georgia, is arguably the capital of the New South. With its four million residents, the second busiest airport in the United States, and traffic jams that rival L.A.'s, Atlanta is an urban giant.

Yet only one hour due north, in the foothills of the Blue Ridge Mountains, is the most idyllic, unusual eighty-seven acres imaginable—a wildlife preserve that contains the largest collection of kangaroos outside of Australia.

The Kangaroo Conservation Center in Dawsonville, Georgia, is the creation of Roger and Debbie Nelson. Roger's interest in animals stems from his youth spent on a farm; Debbie worked at a zoo before attending college. Together they started raising animals in the early 1980s—mostly deer, llamas, and antelopes for zoos. They soon discovered, however, that many zoos were having trouble getting kangaroos because of Australia's strict export policies regarding exotic animals. An idea was born.

Seventeen years later, the Kangaroo Conservation Center keeps approximately two hundred "roos" on the property, and more than 90 percent of them were born there. "We love animals and are interested in educating the public and protecting species," said Debbie. "Most people are surprised when they visit us. They can't believe there are this many kangaroos in Georgia."

The Nelsons offer tours of the facility from early spring through late fall. Tours generally last two hours and are limited to fifty-five people. Safari trucks take

The largest kangaroo collection outside of Australia is in North Georgia.

visitors through about forty acres—where mobs of kangaroos live in a natural setting—before returning to the center's animal care building, where visitors can ask questions and get close to the animals.

Despite their lovable appearance and their gentle natures, kangaroos are very strong and can be dangerous. Adult male red kangaroos are often five to eight feet tall and weigh as much as two hundred pounds; females tend to be about one-third the size of males. In addition to the reds, the Kangaroo Conservation Center has eastern grays, western grays, and dama wallabies, or miniature kangaroos.

Kangaroos can be gentle unless provoked.

A common misconception is that because they box each other kangaroos are aggressive. In fact, male kangaroos box only to determine who will be the leader of the mob. There is usually only one male per mob. "If a kangaroo is threatened," explained Roger, "its basic instinct is to hop away."

Legend suggests that even the common name of the species was based on a misconception. When English explorer Captain James Cook first visited Australia, he supposedly asked the Aborigines what they called the unusual animals hopping around. They answered, "Kangaroo," so Cook returned to England and told everyone about the kangaroos. In the Aboriginal language, however, *kangaroo* meant, "I don't understand." The Aboriginal name for the animals was *marlo*.

Adult kangaroos are fully capable of jumping over the twelve-foot-high fence that surrounds the Kangaroo Conservation Center (they can jump about twelve feet

Contentment in North Georgia

vertically; thirty to forty feet in a horizontal leap), but the animals are so content with their care and surroundings that they do not break out.

Kangaroos are marsupials, meaning they are mammals that lack a placenta and have an external abdominal pouch containing the teats. The gestation period for a kangaroo is approximately thirty days. When a "joey" is born, it is only about the size of a lima bean. It climbs down into its mother's pouch and attaches to a teat, where it remains for the next four months. Depending on the species, the joey will peek out of its mother's pouch at about eight months old, and leave the pouch at about eleven months. A kangaroo's lifespan averages from ten to twenty years.

As an added feature, the Nelsons can teach their visitors how to throw a boomerang . . . maybe in hopes that they, too, will come back.

Debbie Nelson massages a "joey."

Chapter 2

Hell on Wheels

IN A WORLD OF LIP-SYNCING, PREPARED statements, and cosmetic surgery, it's often difficult to find a true-blue original. But anyone who ever met Robert Glenn Johnson Jr. knew immediately that they were confronting "the real thing."

Who?

You may recognize him better by his popular name—Junior Johnson, auto racer supreme and "The Last American Hero," according to writer Tom Wolfe.

Long before Dale Earnhardt was nicknamed "the Intimidator" and even before Richard Petty was crowned "King," Junior Johnson was the most daring, hell-bent, flat-out, belly-to-the-ground driver

Junior behind the wheel

on the nascent stock car racing circuit. "I couldn't stand anybody being ahead of me if my car was capable of being there," Johnson said of his hard-charging style. "I went for the front every time, and I stayed there until I won or blowed up."

There's a lot of mischief in Junior's smile.

As a driver, Johnson won fifty NASCAR events—good enough for a top-ten position on the all-time win list—before retiring in 1966 at age thirty-four at the top of his sport. Subsequently, as an owner his cars won 119 races and six NASCAR Winston Cup Series championships. But Johnson's greatest contributions to racing weren't victories; they were two racing techniques and a fruitful introduction.

Junior Johnson was born June 28, 1931, in Ingle Hollow, North Carolina, a small community outside of Ronda, not far from North Wilkesboro, in the Brushy Mountains in the northwest corner of the state. He lists Ronda (population 460 in the 2000 census) as his hometown, and he was later dubbed "the Ronda Roadrunner" by the racing media.

Times were hard during the Great Depression years of his youth. A little hardscrabble farming kept food on family tables, but making white whiskey from corn was the major enterprise of the region. Writer Vance Packard called Wilkes County "the bootleg capital of America," and Junior Johnson's father was probably the county's leading producer of moonshine.

Junior started driving his father's pickup truck before he was ten, and by age fourteen he was delivering 'shine all over the mountains, driving narrow dirt back roads rather than the more heavily patrolled main highways.

"On moonlight nights, we wouldn't even turn on the headlights. We'd just travel up and down the roads without any lights," remembered Johnson. "And a lot of times you'd meet another bootlegger going the other way, doing the same thing."

Junior soon gained a reputation as

A small, homemade still

one of the best whiskey runners in the state and is often credited with inventing the "bootleg turn," where the driver slams the car into second gear while turning hard left, forcing the car to spin 180 degrees. Many a revenuer saw Junior Johnson

Valuable lessons from dirt roads

in his headlights, but not one ever caught him.

"We took a lot of pride in having the fastest cars," Johnson said. "I had a Ford coupe that would run over a hundred miles an hour; that was unbelievable back in those days. That car would outrun its own sound."

Johnson drove his first race at age eighteen at the nearby North Wilkesboro Raceway. As the legend goes, he was plowing barefooted when his brother, L. P., suggested he enter a fill-in race that night. It didn't take a lot of thought to figure out that racing would be more fun than plowing, so Junior grabbed his shoes and headed for the track. He finished second. The hook was set, and he was soon racing throughout the state.

Johnson built his reputation as a dirt-track demon with driving maneuvers he had developed while outrunning the law. "My style took right off from what I did in the moonshine business," explained Junior. "I learned how to handle a car sideways, backwards, any way you could put it, and get it back where I had control of it."

The "bootleg turn" wasn't of much use on an oval track, but the technique was modified for racing application. Junior never took his foot off the gas heading into a curve, instead he allowed the rear end of the car to slide through the curve and come out with the nose facing down the straightaway. The "power slide" soon became a standard tactic in dirt-track racing.

NASCAR, founded in 1947 by former mechanic and dirt-track-racer-turned-promoter Bill France, had gained the support of automotive manufacturers by the mid 1950s. Pure Oil and Champion Sparkplugs were regular advertisers, and Ford, Chevrolet, and Chrysler all paid the top drivers to race their cars; the advertising slogan of the day was "Race on Sunday, Sell on Monday" since the cars on the track were basically still "stock."

"Bill France Sr. was good friends with lots of ex-bootleggers because they brought a lot to the table for him. A good bootlegger is a racecar driver 99 percent of the time," recalled Johnson. "I was still a young boy and he was trying to talk me into running all the races, but I was still making more money running moonshine than I was racing.

"One morning at breakfast he was asking me to commit to racing full time. I looked over and noticed he was eating bacon and eggs. And I said, 'Mr. France, I'm not committed to running all your races—I'm just involved. Now you see, them eggs you're eating, the hen that laid them was involved. But that bacon you're eating, that pig was committed. I'm not committed.' Almost every time I would see him after that he would ask, 'Are you committed or are you involved?' And I'd answer, 'I'm still involved.'"

As a newcomer to professional racing, Junior Johnson didn't have any corporate sponsors, but he nonetheless won five races during the 1955 season. Fans were attracted to the brash young "giant slayer" from the North Carolina backwoods.

Nineteen fifty-six should have been a big year for Johnson. In fact, he was doing so well at racing that he had nearly decided to back out of the family moonshine business and commit to racing full time. Unfortunately, he waited too long. On May 31, 1956, federal agents—who had never been able to catch him on the roads—arrested him in the woods at his father's still.

Junior's getaway car

"My group leader had a real obsession about nailing the great Junior Johnson," remembered Sid Carter, a former North Carolina highway patrolman who led the raid. "The strategy was to put men all around on one side, then send one man in on the opposite side to flush the suspect toward us. I heard the flush man say, 'Federal officers! You're under arrest!' and then I heard him say, 'Junior, don't hit me with that shovel.' Next thing I heard was a *wham!* and then somebody groaning."

Junior's version of the story was a little different: "I looked up and saw this guy standing on a box about to jump on my back. I had a shovel in my hand at the time, and I throwed it back on my shoulder and it hit him. All I was trying to do was get rid of that shovel and get a head start, you know. And I heard him holler real loud, 'Catch Junior Johnson! He just hit me with a shovel!' But I didn't hit him . . . I just give it to him."

Carter said he chased Junior three- or four-hundred yards before he caught and tackled him. "It was a serious thing, but it was also a fun thing," recalled Carter. "I never knew of any bootleggers trying to hurt revenuers or revenuers trying to hurt bootleggers. It was a competition kind of thing, where you were out to catch them if you could and they were trying to get away if they could."

Johnson was sentenced to two years in the federal reformatory at Chillicothe, Ohio. He served eleven months before being released. (In 1986 President Ronald Reagan granted Junior a presidential pardon, officially wiping his record clean.)

A stock car of yesteryear

Returning to racing in 1958, this time as "committed" as the pig, he won six times and settled into life as a professional racer. "I could work four or five hours a week [racing] and not have to go to jail," reasoned Johnson. He won another five races in 1959, but his breakout came in 1960 at the recently opened Daytona International Speedway.

Johnson did not have a corporate sponsored ride for the 1960 season. Independent owner Ray Fox solicited Johnson to drive his Chevrolet in the second Daytona 500. Fords and Pontiacs were the dominant cars in practice, running ten to fifteen miles per hour faster than Johnson's Chevy, but he was determined to stick to the faster cars as long as he could. Junior told racing writer Orlena Miller what happened next:

> I went out for a practice run, and Fireball Roberts was out there in a Pontiac and I got in right behind him on a curve, right on his bumper. I knew I couldn't stay with him on the straightaway, but I came out of the curve fast, right in behind him, running flat out, and then I noticed a funny thing. As long as I stayed right in behind him, I picked up speed and stayed right with him. My car was going faster than it had ever gone before. It felt like the car was plumb off the ground, floating along.

Junior Johnson had discovered "drafting," the aerodynamic principle that revolutionized auto racing. When two or more cars drive nose-to-tail in a single file, the cars share the same "pocket of air," thus reducing drag and allowing them to travel faster than either could if they were driving alone.

During the race, Johnson stayed on the bumper of the Pontiacs every chance he got. When they pitted, he pitted. Late in the race Johnson pulled ahead and eventually won by twenty-three seconds to record the biggest victory of his career. Fans went wild for the hard-charging Carolinian who had beaten the factory-supported teams. In his 1965 *Esquire* magazine article, Tom Wolfe wrote that after that race "Junior Johnson was like Robin Hood or Jesse James or David." For the rest of the '60 season, he was the man to beat. It is said that the Ford Motor Company spent five million dollars that season trying to catch Junior Johnson.

The "Ronda Roadrunner" won another thirty-three races over the next five years, including thirteen races during 1965, his final season. Almost poetically, his last victory as a driver came on October 3, 1965, at North Wilkesboro, often called "the house that Junior built," just a few miles from where his storied driving career had begun.

As a car owner, Junior Johnson won more races than any other owner in the history of the sport except for Richard Petty Enterprises. His list of drivers included some of the top names in NASCAR history: Fred Lorenzen, Curtis Turner, Lee Roy Yarborough, Bobby Allison, Cale Yarborough, Darrell Waltrip, and Terry Labonte. Johnson sold the team in 1995 and permanently retired to his cattle farm near North Wilkesboro.

But Johnson's most significant contribution to auto racing may have been an introduction he made in 1970, the year that tobacco advertising was banned from television.

NASCAR teams were losing support from Ford and Chrysler, and Johnson, like many car owners, was searching for sponsorship dollars. He approached R. J. Reynolds, the tobacco giant based in his home state, about sponsoring his racing team. During those conversations, Johnson discovered that Reynolds was looking for an effective place for the millions of advertising dollars previously targeted for TV. He shrewdly introduced R. J. Reynolds to Bill France, founder and CEO of NASCAR, and the two renegades formed a perfect union that became the Winston Cup Series.

Once R. J. Reynolds demonstrated that racing fans—brand loyal and basically untapped by Madison Avenue—were a strong audience, a variety of industries took notice. Soon laundry detergents, beer, coffee, and other commercial products were being advertised on the sides of race cars. Today NASCAR is one of the most effective means of targeted advertising in America. And much of the credit for that success belongs to Robert Glenn Johnson Jr. of North Wilkesboro, North Carolina—"The Last American Hero."

Chapter 3

The Real Jack Daniel

"I don't drink. I don't like it. It makes me feel good."
—*Oscar Levant,* 1906–1972

THERE'S AN OLD SAYING THAT SOMETIMES A MAN has to drink to make other folks seem interesting. Well, no one has to be tippling anything to make the man behind "Old No. 7"—Tennessee's legendary sour mash whiskey—a fascinating character.

The larger-than-life real Jack Daniel was not much taller in physical stature than the white oak barrels in which he aged his liquor. Measuring just five feet two inches tall, the little big man wore a size four shoe. Years after his death, when a statue was created of him for the company distillery in Lynchburg, the

Life-size statute . . .
except for the feet.

21

sculptor had to make Jack's boots larger than they would have been in reality so that the life-size statue wouldn't topple over.

Those who know a thing or two about sipping whiskey probably won't be surprised that Jasper "Jack" Newton Daniel was of Scotch-Irish descent. His forefathers had settled in Franklin County in southeastern Tennessee in the early 1800s when the area was still mostly wilderness. A man needed plenty of pluck to make it in those days, and Jack—who was born on a Moore County farm in the early fall of 1846—had plenty of it from the start.

He was the youngest child in Lucinda and Calloway Daniel's large family, and his mother died only months after he was born. When his father remarried a few years later, and most of the attention went to the new stepmother and Jack's many brothers and sisters (some say there were as many as thirteen siblings), he promptly decided to leave the family home and move in with a neighbor. He had just turned six years old.

At age seven he was working for the Reverend Daniel Houston Call at Call's General Store. A storekeeper's inventory of that era had to include everything the locals needed: flour, sugar, spices, fabric, thread, pins, needles, medicines, shoes, tools, utensils, and *whiskey*. Dan Call was a Lutheran man of God, but he also successfully ran a makeshift distillery on Louise Creek. By eight, Jack was working at the still.

The Reverend taught young Jack Daniel all the important things in life—honesty, hard work, and the sour mash process of making spirits. Much like making sourdough bread, making "sour mash" necessitates that a portion of the previous batch is retained so that it can be used as the "starter" for the next. The method uses natural fermentation, speeds up the fomentation of ingredients, and guarantees consistency.

As Call's apprentice, Jack also learned the Tennessee "Lincoln County" process of mellowing the liquor, where sugar maple is burned into charcoal; the newly made whiskey is then slowly poured through giant containers that are "hard-packed" with ten feet of the charred wood. According to company literature, the method takes ten days and "during this time the whiskey absorbs the essence of the charcoal and gives the drink its distinctive taste and aroma."

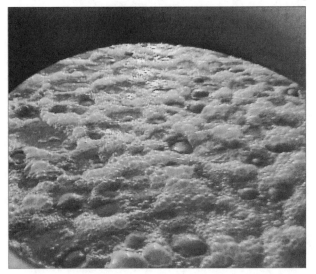

Legend has it that when Jack was in his early teens, a female evangelist at a camp revival meeting delivered a fire-and-brimstone sermon that caused Dan Call's wife to present the good preacher with an ultimatum: you can make the devil's brew or you can save souls, but you can't do both. So at age thirteen, Jack purchased the "business" from Reverand Call.

The frothy brew that will become Old No. 7

"One Call [descendant] wished he'd given up preaching instead," wrote Peter Krass in the 2004 biography, *Blood & Whiskey: The Life and Times of Jack Daniel*, "because the Jack Daniel Distillery was eventually worth tens of millions of dollars."

Part of that success came from the fact that Jack Daniel was a public relations and marketing genius, using hot air balloons and the Jack Daniel's Original Silver Cornet Band to attract attention and headlines. He also designed special commemorative bottles and the distinctive square-shaped, black-labeled bottle that made his product stand out from all the others.

The distinctive square bottle

But it was the special spirits that were poured inside those bottles that really gained attention. Made from pure, mineral-free spring water that flows from a limestone cave that Jack found, and then aged in barrels that, according to Master Distiller Jimmy Bedford, give the whiskey "all of its color and some of its flavor," Jack Daniel's Old No. 7 Brand Old-Time Tennessee Sour Mash Whiskey tastes like nothing else.

There are countless legends about how Jack decided on the exact recipe and the name that soon became internationally famous. "You can talk to twenty employees here at the distillery," said Roger Brashears, "and get seventeen different reasons why he picked 'Old No. 7.'"

"I [think I] know the real story of where Old No. 7 came from," claimed his great-grandniece, Lynn Tolley. "At the turn of the [twentieth] century, there was a World's Fair Exposition in St. Louis, Missouri. At that time you could enter whiskey into the competition. So Jack Daniel tasted seven barrels of whiskey. The seventh barrel he thought was the best. And that is the one that he sent to St. Louis. It won the gold medal."

"I personally think that after trying seven different recipes, he liked the seventh recipe the best," said Randall Fanning, a tour guide at the distillery.

Aging in barrels adds color, flavor.

"I always like the story that he had seven girlfriends at one time, him being a bachelor," said Brashears. "But I think I made that one up, so I don't put much faith in it."

Although he never married and was never known to have had a great love, Jack Daniel was indeed known as a ladies' man. When he died in 1911 at age sixty-one, he was buried in the cemetery at Lynchburg. But so many of "his girlfriends were going there to *weep*," said Lynne Tolley, "that [the family] decided to put two little wrought iron chairs right in front of the tombstone."

"They've been there ever since he was buried," claimed Brashears. "The common lore around here is there was so many ladies that didn't get to marry him" that the chairs were placed at Jack's gravesite "to help them over their bereavement."

"There were ladies lying on the ground," said Fanning. "They put the chairs there so that they'd at least get to sit and cry."

Yes, "he was quite a dandy," said his niece; he sported a sweeping black mustache and beard and "he always wore boots. We think that gave him a little extra height."

"He was a very classy little fellow," added Brashears. And when he turned twenty-one—which in Jack Daniel years was equal to an average man's first forty—he went on a shopping spree that determined his dapper look for rest of his life. He returned from the excursion wearing a wide-brimmed planter's

Still a ladies' man after all these years

hat and a formal black "frock coat" that came to his knees. There was a small black tie at his neck and a gold key chain hanging at his waist just below the vest. Later, out of necessity, he added a cane. The outfit became as much a trademark and as uniquely Jack's as his whiskey's square bottle.

Jack and his name were famous. He was making big money. And he owned the oldest federally registered distillery in the country.

But strong spirits rarely come without a few explosions.

"Mr. Jack Daniel may not have been hot tempered," said Roger Brashears, "but he was sort of set in his ways. And he came in [to work] one morning, and he just couldn't get the combination to the safe to work. He flew mad and kicked it, broke the big toe on his left foot."

Without a doctor's attention, gangrene soon set in and the injured toe had to be amputated. Eventually, so did the foot and part of his leg. Although it was a few years before the infection spread and proved deadly, that one angry kick killed old Jack.

If you go to Lynchburg today, employees of the distillery will be pleased to give you a tour of the internationally known company that a Tennessee teenager made famous. You can also sit for a spell in one of the wrought iron chairs next to Jack's grave. But don't expect to raise a shot of Old No. 7 in his honor. Lynchburg has been officially "dry" since 1909, and you'll have to cross the county line to do any serious sipping.

Chapter 4

The Murphy Village Travelers

SOUTHERN BOYS AND GIRLS GROW UP HEARING THEIR MOTHERS' ADMONITION that "A good reputation takes years to build, and a bad reputation takes years to erase." If they ever need an example, the Irish Travelers of Murphy Village, South Carolina, would be quintessential proof of that warning.

Since they first arrived in America more than 150 years ago—fleeing poverty and famine in their home country of Ireland—Travelers have been trying to change their stereotypical reputation as "gypsies, tramps, and thieves." But it's hard to change an opinion that has been built over centuries.

Scholars speculate that the Travelers descended from a nomadic race of pre-Celtic minstrels and poets who roamed Great Britain more than two thousand years ago. Oliver Cromwell—who would become Lord Protector of England, Scotland, and Ireland—added to the ranks of Travelers in 1649 when he led a bloody campaign through Ireland; by confiscating 40 percent of the land of Ireland from Irish Catholics and giving it to British Protestants, he created an instant class of vagabonds. Two

Irish immigrants flocked to America in the 1850s.

hundred years later, the Irish famine of 1846–50 claimed a million lives from hunger and disease; generations of emigrants, including the "Traveling People," came to the United States with nothing, hoping for a new start. But their reception was hardly warm: no group was considered lower than Irishmen in America during the 1850s.

The offer of free land on the new American frontier was not attractive to the Irish; they had seen how easily land could be taken away and how blighted it could become. So they settled in cities, overcrowded and cloistered; almost all large U.S. cities had an "Irish Town" or "Shanty Town." The *Chicago Post* wrote, "The Irish fill our prisons, our poorhouses . . . Scratch a convict or a pauper, and the chances are that you tickle the skin of an Irish Catholic."

The Irish Travelers escaped the city and returned to their nomadic roots. They roamed from town to town in decorated, horse-drawn carts, often earning money by mending pots, kettles, and pans and as tinsmiths, just as their ancestors had done. Consequently, they were sometimes called "Tinkers," but that term is considered a slur today (as is the misnomer "White Gypsies," since the Travelers are not Gypsies but a distinctly different group). They also became skilled horse and mule traders, and after that trade died out, they specialized in itinerant sales of goods and services.

The Travelers stuck together as a means of protection and to guard their culture. They played the old music and practiced storytelling. They spoke dialects of Shelta (also known as Gammon or Cant), a secret language with roots back to the thirteenth century that includes elements of Irish Gaelic, English, Greek, and Hebrew. They also remained devout Roman Catholics who rarely married outside their group.

By 1900, Travelers were common sights across the South, albeit not always welcomed sights. A rural Georgia newspaper wrote of them: "One would be advised to check the paint on the door posts before the next rains, see that the floral pattern on the dining room floor covering remains true, and even look closely at the new pony's shade of brown. Be advised."

The Travelers had a ritualistic connection to Atlanta, as described by Msgr. Noel C. Burtenshaw of the Catholic Archdiocese of Atlanta in a 1986 article:

For many years April 28 was a most important date for these travelers. On that date they would gather at the Shrine of the Immaculate Conception in downtown Atlanta for their annual funeral service. Since they continued a set pilgrimage throughout the year, should a member of the clan die, the remains were sent to an Atlanta funeral home and kept until that April date. Then, like a swarming army, the clan would gather and all the caskets would be brought to the Immaculate for the funeral mass. Often there were five or six caskets in the sanctuary on that day. Burial would then take place at Oakland cemetery. The graves and the plots are there to be seen to this day.

The Traveler tradition of once-a-year burials ended in the early 1960s—about the same time that modernity finally caught up with the Irish nomads.

Full-time life on the road had become unsustainable and the Travelers needed a

Travelers held an annual burial service.

base. In 1966, Father Joseph Murphy, a parish priest and advocate, convinced them to buy fifty acres of land near St. Edward's Catholic Church in North Augusta, South Carolina, as a "home." Approximately three hundred families settled there and subsequently named their community Murphy Village in his honor. Other groups of Travelers formed communities in White Settlement, Texas, and Memphis, Tennessee. For the first time in a millennium, "the walking people" had taken root.

Ornate trailers were parked and replaced by trucks and vans, and people who had never had a home started building houses. "When I first moved to Aiken County, I heard about the Gypsies, and everybody said, 'You need to go see their houses,'" recalled Phyllis Brit, a longtime resident. "They had lots of religious statues in the yards, but the most unusual thing was that some of the houses had aluminum foil over the windows. I think it was some sort of tradition about keeping out evil spirits. But otherwise they were just normal people who prefer to keep to themselves. These

Religious shrines are commonplace.

are not the tambourine-hitting kinds of Gypsies. They live in the twenty-first century but hold on to centuries-old traditions."

The main tradition that has continued is that the men still head out each spring for six to eight months on the road, working as painters, roofers, pavers, carpenters, and salesmen until the onset of winter. "They like their trucks and basically live in them for large parts of the year," said resident Mim Woodring. Although some wives travel with their husbands, most women with school-age children remain at home. Modern Traveler children usually attend school only through the sixth or seventh grade.

Aluminum foil over the windows repels spirits.

"Formal education has never been as important to us as domestic life," explained one Traveler (they prefer not to be identified). "Our girls want to get married and care for their families, and our boys want to start working." Woodring remembered, "When I was in high school at North Augusta, one of the Traveler girls actually graduated with us. We all applauded her because that was so unusual."

But while many things have changed, many have remained the same. Travelers still think of themselves as nomads and their houses as temporary lodging. They have remained a very tightly knit community, because many of their mores are un-acceptable among "the settled" or "country people," their names for non-Travelers. For example, marriage takes place only within the clan, meaning close relatives sometimes marry. Today in Murphy Village there are approximately three thousand Travelers (the largest enclave in the United States) but fewer than a dozen surnames—Costello, O'Hara, Riley, Sherlock, Carroll, McNamara, and Gorman are the most common. And most marriages are still arranged by parents and include a sizeable dowry.

Very young girls, as young as ten to twelve years old, can be married according to Traveler custom.

"Family is very important to us," said one Traveler. "You'll never find a Traveler in a nursing home, and it's impossible to find an orphan."

Unfortunately, what often calls attention to the publicity-shy Travelers is their reputation for scamming people. The most frequent scams are related to home improvement projects, where Travelers start the job, get an advance or a deposit, and then vanish. Pursuing the wrongdoers is particularly difficult because so many of them share the same last names and are best known by nicknames.

"That's the only way we can distinguish between ourselves," explained a Traveler. But it's particularly difficult for law enforcement officers to pursue "Peekaboo" or "Black Pete" or "Charlie Boy." Even the women have occasionally been caught participating in a flimflam. The most common is stealing merchandise and then returning it for cash. "We're like any other community," said one Traveler. "We've got good people and bad people. A few yonks [thieves] can spoil it for the rest of us."

The Irish Travelers, estimated at between fifteen and twenty thousand today in the United States, try to live below society's radar. A long history of persecution and misconception has left them suspicious of "country people." As one Traveler said, "We are the survivors of a long line of our people. We just want to be left alone to live our lives as we see fit."

Chapter 5

The Bell Witch

Witch in the Glass

My mother says I must not pass
Too near that glass;
She is afraid that I will see
A little witch that looks like me,
With a red mouth to whisper low
The very thing I should not know.

—*Sarah Morgan Bryant Piatt*

ON THE FAR SIDE OF BELLWOOD CEMETERY, ON THE OUTSKIRTS OF TINY Adams, Tennessee, is a family burial plot where John Bell has been resting for more than 180 years. Situated near the Red River approximately thirty miles northwest of Nashville and less than ten miles from the Kentucky state line, the area is surrounded by Tennessee hills and old forests. Standing at the edge of the Bell family plot is a monument to John Bell, his wife, Lucy, and their nine children. The setting is quiet and peaceful, almost serene. Unfortunately, the lives of John and his family were anything but that.

John Bell, Jr., witnessed his father's harassment.

After several years of prosperity as a planter in Edgecombe County, North Carolina, John Bell suffered two or three seasons of failed crops. Hoping that farming conditions might be more favorable if he moved west, Bell decided to relocate. In December 1803, John and Lucy and their four young sons made the arduous trip across North Carolina and the East Tennessee mountains and settled in what at that time was called Red River Station. The rich bottomland of central Tennessee was a perfect place for growing the crops that are still harvested there today: corn and tobacco. By all measures, moving to such fertile land was a wise decision, and Bell had every reason to believe that he and his growing family would thrive in their new home.

And for the first fifteen years they farmed the Tennessee frontier, the Bells did indeed thrive. Lucy, who was twenty years John's junior, gave birth to five more children, and the family moved into a large log house and eventually purchased additional tracts of land adjacent to their property. John was named a deacon of their church and Lucy, although she was illiterate, was considered one of the most intelligent people in Red River Station. Father and sons tilled the land, crops were plentiful, and the Bells became one of the most prosperous families in the section of Tennessee now known as Robertson County.

Their luck began to change, though, in 1817, and the family became afflicted in ways they could never have imagined.

"It was then that they started hearing noises on the exterior portion of the house," according to historian Eugene Davidson, "which within a few weeks manifested itself to come inside."

The trouble began the night after John Bell had been out walking in one of his cornfields and spotted a bizarre-looking animal. "It looked like a dog in a way, but it also looked like a rabbit," said Patrick A. Fitzhugh, an historian and author of numerous books, including one titled *Bell Witch: The Full Account*. "He didn't know what it was and he was just baffled."

John Bell did what most men would have done in those days: he raised his rifle. Although he fired several shots, he missed each time and the animal disappeared.

That night the family began to hear beating and knocking sounds on the outside walls. The noises continued over the next few nights, always growing in intensity. Each time John and his sons ran outdoors expecting to find the cause, they found nothing amiss and no one prowling around the house.

"As the legend goes," said Fitzhugh, "they got to where they were very scared to go out after dark, and a little while after that the children started

The old Bell house saw many unusual happenings.

feeling their bedcovers pulled back. Pillows were jerked out from under them, and one of the daughters, Elizabeth, even got slapped by invisible hands."

The noises increased, and the children heard scratching sounds at the foot of their beds. Different members of the family were kicked and pinched. Along with the scratching and banging sounds, a female voice also began to be heard. At first the voice was faint and sounded as if it came from an elderly woman. With time the voice grew stronger, sometimes singing hymns and other times crying and swearing. Twelve-year-old Elizabeth, or Betsy, as the family called her, was the child who took the brunt of the treatment and was pricked and jabbed with pins and something repeatedly yanked and pulled at her hair.

Despite the strange disturbances going on in her house, Betsy Bell grew up, fell in love, and became engaged to a neighbor, Joshua Gardner. But the haunting continued, and the spirit or ghost or "witch," as she soon was called, warned Betsy over and over not to marry Gardner; the young couple was so constantly harassed that Betsy eventually called off the wedding.

Author Fitzhugh has written that "Kate," as the spirit was sometimes called, was a "supernatural entity." Dr. Nandor Fodor, a psychologist and author from the nineteenth century, believed that the haunting was a result of poltergeists connected to Betsy. Fodor also claimed that the Bell Witch was "America's greatest ghost story."

Whatever "she" or "it" was, the patriarch of the family was the soul who was afflicted the most unmercifully. Around 1818, according to Patrick Fitzhugh, "John Bell began having problems he described as his feeling like there was a piece of wood stuck in his mouth holding his cheeks apart. He had trouble with swallowing, and the condition worsened over time. All during this time the spirit was saying, 'I am here to kill John Bell, and I will see him to a very agonizing and grisly death.'"

This was a time of great spirituality in the South, and what started as the Red River Revival became an annual event that brought thousands of people to nearby

Johnston's Campground on Sturgeon Creek. It was also only a few generations removed from the witch trials of New England, and anything that had to do with the occult or witchcraft was considered sinister and evil. Although John Bell had once been a leader in his church, he was eventually excommunicated. It isn't known for certain whether he was thrown out of the congregation because of the fast-spreading news of a spirit's association with the family, or because of what some in the valley said was John's connection to a questionable business deal.

Whatever the cause, the old man's torment continued. "In October of 1820, according to research, John and his youngest son went out to separate some hogs," said Patrick Fitzhugh. "And while they were walking, John Bell's shoes started flying off. And then he was slapped, according to the legend. He would get his shoes on [and] they would come off and some invisible hand would slap him in the face and knock him all the way to the ground. Legend has it that he never left the house again."

Soon after that he began suffering from what many now believe was a neurological disease, with symptoms that included headaches and seizures. Finally, on December 19, 1820, John Bell fell into a coma and died early the next day.

Beside the dead man's bed, his family found a small bottle containing a dark, mysterious liquid. When one of the sons placed a drop of the foul-smelling stuff on the tongue of a cat, the animal immediately died. "This voice spoke up," said Fitzhugh, "and said, 'Oh, I gave Ol' Jack Bell a dose of that last night. It was a big dose that I finally fixed him.'"

At his funeral, the voice purportedly laughed, sang, and cheerfully claimed credit for John Bell's passing. According to Fitzhugh, Bell "is the only person in history whose death was attributed to the doings of a spirit."

His widow, Lucy Bell, inherited the farm and its buildings. But years later it was subdivided and dispersed among her heirs. "More subdivisions occurred," said Fitzhugh, "and one particular tract of land which has some significance is a cave tract."

Bell Witch Cave

Chris Kirby and her husband own what has for some time been referred to as Bell Witch Cave, which is on a bluff on the northwest corner of the original Bell farm. "Just after we moved in here," said Kirby, "we started hearing strange things that we couldn't find a logical explanation for. Weird things coming up on [photographs] that couldn't be explained and just, you know, a lot of things . . . like the dog and cat would act up in the cave: barking and growling and the cat hissing and blowing. Nothing there, you know."

The entrance to unexplained occurrences.

Patrick Fitzhugh also wrote about several unexplained incidents that have occurred in the cave. One in particular "involved a little boy who accidentally got his head stuck between two rocks. After the boy yelled for some time, the entire cave lit up and invisible hands tugged at his legs. His head was free and he was pulled all the way back to the cave entrance."

Candy Kirby, who helps her parents give tours in the cave, said, "There's a lot of different types of things that happen. Some make you feel scared. Others make you feel comfortable—believe it or not."

There are claims that snakes have been found hanging from the site's entrance gates and that noises sometimes come from deep within the cave. But Candy Kirby said that the most common occurrences are voices: "Normally you're standing in the first room and you hear something on back in the cave. You know, it sounds like two men talking or mumbling back and forth to each other."

Eerie noises have been heard from inside the cave.

The Rabbit-Dog Creature

Some versions of the Bell Witch story say there is a connection between the haunting and John Bell's taking aim at the strange half-rabbit, half-dog creature that first appeared the day the banging and voices started. "It's very widely known in the legend that a rabbit was the spirit's most favorite form of manifestation," said Fitzhugh.

Carney Bell, a descendant of the John Bell family, agreed with Fitzhugh. "I have four boys, and I was taking them hunting one day," said Bell, "and there was a farm not too far from here and I took them out on the farm and we were hunting rabbits. And we jumped a rabbit and two or three of the boys shot at it, and I guess it rolled in the thicket. I put my hand on what I thought was a tree stump. When I looked at the stump, it wasn't a stump at all. It was a cemetery monument. It was Joel Ingrid Bell's grave, my great grandfather, who was the baby in the family."

The Bell Witch came back once, as promised, in 1828. When she did she spoke mainly to John Bell Jr. and prophesied many things, including the Civil War, the Great Depression, and the World Wars.

She also said she would return again in a little more than a hundred years and visit John Bell's descendants. The year she was supposed to have returned was 1935; as far as family members know, she never paid the visit. But others say that her presence can still be felt in the area, and some like Patrick Fitzhugh have asked if she ever left at all.

"One night in the 1950s," he said, "three teenage boys from Nashville visited the old Bell cemetery in Adams and decided to lift John Bell's tombstone and put it in the back of their car and take it home with them. On the way home, they had a terrible wreck. The driver was killed instantly and within two weeks the other two passengers, who were not hurt in the accident, both died strange deaths."

There are little more than five hundred residents in Adams today. The railroad track runs through the middle of town, and the sleepy Bellwood Cemetery is on land that was part of the original Bell family farm. Less than a half mile away, in front of the red brick Bell School, there's a marker put up by the Tennessee Historical Commission that gives a brief explanation of the Bell Witch haunting. Each August hundreds come to town to enjoy the Bell Witch Bluegrass Festival, and tourists come year-round to take pictures of John Bell's grave and peek inside the cool, eerie Bell Witch cave.

Is the spirit that tormented the Bells for so long indeed still around?

Standing near John Bell Jr.'s tombstone, historian Davidson didn't say. But he admitted that "people have picked up rocks or stones or objects" from the Bell property, but "for whatever reason, they brought them back."

"I don't know how to explain it," Chris Kirby said. "I know there's something here, but what it actually is, I don't know."

"There's definitely something in this cave," added her daughter Candy.

"There's something here," agreed Chris.

Chapter 6

The Edgar Watson Murder

THE ONLY PEOPLE WHO WENT TO SOUTHWEST FLORIDA IN THE EARLY 1890s were running away from something or someone. Edgar Watson—one of the most infamous men among Florida's early white settlers—was no exception.

Calusa, Miccosukee, and Seminole Native Americans had lived on the land for hundreds of years. In fact, the Calusa were direct descendants of Paleo-Indians who first inhabited southwest Florida twelve thousand years earlier, when the climate was much colder and the landmass extended another sixty miles into the Gulf of Mexico. By the 1600s, the Calusa had created habitable islands with huge mounds of shells, which led to their being called "Shell People" by early settlers.

Ed Watson's Everglades

Mound Key, today a 125-acre island in Estero Bay north of Naples, is such an island.

Partially because of their protein-rich diet of seafood, the Calusa were typically six to twelve inches taller than the Spaniards who began settling Florida in the 1600s, but their health was no match for European diseases. An estimated twenty thousand Calusa lived in South Florida when the Spanish arrived; by the time the English gained control of Florida in 1763, only a few hundred remained. Most Native Americans who survived the ravages of smallpox and other European diseases were subsequently forced out of Florida during the 1830s under terms of the Indian Removal Act.

Even then, the lower third of the Florida peninsula was considered uninhabitable swamp. The Everglades were a "River of Grass" (so-named by twentieth-century author Marjory Stoneman Douglas) flowing from the Kissimmee River, through Lake Okeechobee in the middle of the state, to the Ten Thousand Islands area off the southwest Florida coast. White settlers first appeared in the region in the 1870s. By the 1880s land speculators began digging drainage canals, creating "new" land but disrupting the ecosystem. Vast stands of mangrove trees along the coast were removed to improve views.

It was to this wild setting—similar to the Wild West that was being settled during that same time—that Edgar Watson came in 1892. The local population consisted mostly of swindlers, Civil War deserters, runaway slaves, and other misfits trying to get lost or looking for a new start. Watson bought a forty-acre, shell-mound island south of Chokoloskee and began growing sugar cane—the number one crop of the boggy region—and winter vegetables. But suspicion grew as fast as his crops.

Watson was born in Edgefield County, South Carolina, in 1855. When he was a young boy, his mother fled with him and his younger sister, Minnie, from her abusive, alcoholic husband. They settled with relatives in Lakeland, Florida. As he grew up, Watson's Scottish descent was mirrored in his red hair, blue eyes, and fiery temper.

He married and fathered a son, but his young wife died shortly thereafter and the son went to live with his mother's family. Watson married again and fathered two more children, but the family was uprooted suddenly one night when Watson loaded them onto a buggy and headed for Arkansas; there were rumors that he was wanted for the murder of his brother-in-law in Florida.

The Arkansas Territory was a dangerous place in the 1880s. Disputes were often settled with firearms, and outlaws threatened what little authority there was. Watson, in fact, had leased some farmland from the notorious Belle Starr, already legendary for her connection to outlaws Cole Younger and Frank and Jesse James, as well as for her own questionable exploits.

Belle was under constant scrutiny by local authorities looking for any reason to arrest her, so when she heard that Watson was a fugitive wanted for murder, she told him he would have to move off her land. A heated dispute ensued. Belle reportedly told Watson, "I don't suppose the United States officers would trouble you, but the Florida officers might." On February 3, 1889, while returning from the general store to her ranch in Eufaula, Oklahoma, Belle Starr was killed by a shotgun blast to the back. Her murderer was never identified, but Watson departed immediately, leaving his family to follow later, for the wilds of southwest Florida.

For the next couple of years, Watson blended in with the other traders and "businessmen"

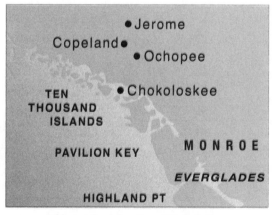

Old map shows location of Chokoloskee.

sending resources from the Everglades down to Key West for shipping. Buttonwood, sometimes called "false mangrove" and used to make charcoal, was a major export at the time. And with the expansive Everglades always at his back, Watson could easily disappear should his past ever get too close. But once again, controversy followed Watson.

"The story was that Watson was in Key West when he came upon Quinn Bass, a broker, cutting up another fellow in a knife fight," said James Sluiter, a park ranger with the Ten Thousand Islands National Wildlife Refuge. "Watson supposedly stepped in and told Bass that he'd done enough, at which time Bass threatened Watson, and Watson shot him dead."

Watson bought his shell-mound island in 1892 and began farming. During the next fifteen years he prospered by building one of the most successful sugarcane-syrup operations in the area. Migrant workers did most of the labor, and rumors persisted that some of them frequently disappeared just before payday, later to be found floating in the marsh or partially eaten by sharks. In the wilds of southwest Florida, no one asked too many questions about things that didn't affect them.

Lake Okeechobee

Meanwhile, southwest Florida experienced its first land boom, as developers dug canals and dredged the swamps to create new tracts of land where none had existed. Freshwater from Lake Okeechobee was diverted, and the ecosystem that had remained unchanged for thousands of years was altered overnight.

Suspicion still drifted to Watson whenever there was trouble. "Watson owned some property on Lostman's Key," explained Sluiter, a student of the history of the area. "Some homesteaders named Tucker set up there, and Watson sent them a letter demanding that they vacate the property. Tucker sent back a terse reply, and shortly thereafter the Tucker clan was found dead."

Finally in the fall of 1910, the townspeople of Chokoloskee Island reached their limit. Watson's reputation for administering "frontier justice" had left them all antsy, wondering who would be next. "Mothers would say to their kids at night, 'If you don't go to sleep, Mr. Watson will come get you.' He had even picked up the nickname of 'The Barber' because he reportedly shot the moustache off a man," said Sluiter. A group confronted him outside the Ted Smallwood Store, which served as a general store, post office, and Indian trading post for the area.

"They questioned him about all the missing workers, and about the death of Hannah Smith, a friend of Watson's who had turned up dead," said Sluiter. "But Watson blamed all the deaths on Leslie Cox, his foreman, who was known to be a bad man. Watson told the group he would take care of Cox himself and bring back his dead body as proof."

A couple of days later, on October 17, 1910, a "big blow" hurricane swamped the entire area. From Key West to Tampa Bay, low-lying buildings were swept away and thirty people died. Residents of shell-mound islands like Chokoloskee Island quickly understood why the Calusa had built them as high as twenty feet above sea level.

Shortly afterward, word came that Edgar Watson was headed back to town. A group of twenty to thirty townspeople, all armed, waited for him where the dock outside Smallwood's Store had been before the storm took it away.

"Watson's boat pulled right up to shore," said Sluiter. "He had Leslie Cox's hat, he said, and showed the crowd a bullet hole through the hat. He told them that he had confronted Cox about the killings, and when Cox admitted them, Watson shot him. The body fell in the water and was lost, but Watson brought the hat as proof. The locals had heard enough, and they say you could hear hammers being cocked throughout the crowd. That's when Watson raised his double-barrel shotgun, aimed it at the crowd, and pulled both triggers. Apparently his paper shells hadn't dried out from the storm, though, because neither barrel fired.

"Everybody on the shore returned fire. Watson was hit thirty to forty times. They left him right where he fell, and his body lay on the beach until the next day. Kids poked it with sticks to be sure he was dead, and his body was looted. They didn't want to bury him in the local cemetery, so they tied a rope around his feet and dragged him five miles to Rabbit Key, where they buried his remains in the sand," Sluiter recounted.

Edgar Watson's life of suspected violence had come to a violent end. And justice—the "frontier" variety or vigilante style—had been served.

Watson's legacy was assured when renowned writer Peter Matthiessen wrote three novels based on the scattered facts of Watson's life. The first volume, *Killing Mr. Watson*, had observers tell about Watson's life and death. The second book, *Lost Man's River*, was the fictionalized account of Watson's son's attempts to understand his father's sordid past. And the final piece, *Bone by Bone*, was the story told by Watson himself.

"Some folks thought he was a good man who helped develop the area," said Sluiter, "but to others he'll always be remembered as the worst of the worse."

Chapter 7

The Pea Island Surfmen

I walked beside the evening sea
And dreamed a dream that could not be;
The waves that plunged along the shore
Said only: "Dreamer, dream no more!"
—*Georgia William Curtis, 1824–1892*

THERE IS A SMALL, WINDSWEPT, CATERPILLAR-SHAPED SECTION OF LAND THAT makes up the northern section of Hatteras Island along North Carolina's Outer Banks. It is known as Pea Island and is a feeding and resting place for more than three hundred species of shorebirds, waterfowl, and other permanent and migratory birds. Raccoons, opossums, muskrats, and river otter feed off the shellfish and small fish in the tidal creeks and ponds here; terrapin, loggerheads, rabbits, and snakes live on the hummocky sand dunes or among the live oaks, marsh grass, and thickets of this barrier island of America's eastern seacoast.

In fair weather, the sun glistens and bobs on the surf, and the white sands reflect so much light they blind the unprotected eye. Wading birds slowly make their high-stepping way along the water's edge and leave hieroglyphic footprints on the beach at low tide. Endangered peregrine falcons can be spotted above, and schools of fish can be seen darting in the waters of Pamlico Sound. Sitting on the beach in late afternoon, with feet in the foam and salt air blowing against one's face, Pea Island is a birder's and naturalist's paradise.

Deadly rip currents off the Outer Banks

But in foul weather, in the dark of night, the unpredictable seashore and strong tides of the Outer Banks can wreak disaster.

Through the centuries so many vessels have lost their way and crashed upon the sandbars and shoals, and so many desperate sailors have tried to jump to safety from their sinking ships only to be caught in the relentless undertow, that this stretch of North Carolina coastline has become known as the "graveyard of the Atlantic."

According to researchers David Wright and David Zoby, the area that has claimed the most ships is the forty-five mile stretch from Oregon Inlet to the tip of Cape Hatteras. Oregon Inlet was named after the *Oregon,* following the hurricane of 1846 that sliced open Bodie Island, leaving the ship stranded on a sandbar in the middle of the newly formed inlet.

In their book *Fire on the Beach,* Wright and Zoby stated that "the frigid, south-ward-flowing Labrador currents collide with the tepid, north-flowing Gulf Stream, forming hidden shoals where depths can go from 125 fathoms to two in just a few yards."

is almost smack in the middle of this unforgiving span of seacoast.

in the early days of America's maritime history traveled past the

cedented numbers because of the fast-moving currents there

time off a voyage. But they continued to do so at their

vessel safety wasn't the responsibility of the United

World War II and for years, once a ship began

little chance of it or its crew being rescued.

ial times are recorded to have sunk upon

crews being lost to the sweeping

water and. So many boats went down,

in fact, th as the "Bankers" referred to

the salvaging nearly every storm and

resulting disaster.

Finally, in 1871, to U.S. Life-Saving
Service was founded by t en then, captains
never knew for certain if the
fewer than two hundred LSS st
were sprinkled along thousands of m
the U.S. coastline would send their patr
into treacherous storms and high, boat-
swamping seas to save a ship.

Particularly during the first years of the LSS,
as Wright and Zoby have written, "a scent of
doom tainted the service," with its "surfmen"
far more famous for their lack of leadership
and professionalism than for their heroism and

Pea Island rescue boat

prowess at recovering shipwrecked sailors. Two of the worst shipping accidents in the 1870s—the downing of the *Huron* and the *Metropolis*—occurred off the Outer Banks and made, as the two historians wrote, "headlines that horrified Americans from coast to coast. There were tales of stations being padlocked and off-limits to fishermen just yards from a ship in distress, of surfmen capsizing their lifeboat and drowning along with the mariners they had come to rescue, of lifesavers rifling through the pockets of victims washed ashore."

But a number of the surfmen of the LSS were honorable and dedicated men who spent the majority of their working lives dutifully patrolling beaches, honing their rowing skills, and enduring all manner of foul weather and hardships.

"These people risked their lives to save others, for very little monetary or social or any other kinds of benefits," said Bob Huggett of North Carolina's Chicamacomico Life-Saving Museum on the Outer Banks. "The surfmen were required to supply their own food and their own clothes. They were paid forty dollars a month in cash. The keeper was paid six hundred dollars a year and he was expected to be there all the time." They spent their days and nights basically in isolation, drilling with military precision and preparing for the worst the sea could throw at them. The keeper and six-member "colored crew" at Pea Island were considered to be the best of the best.

In the winter of 1890, the nation was still recovering—physically, psychologically, politically, and economically—from the ravages of the Civil War. Jobs were scarce along the Outer Banks, especially for former slaves. Chicamacomico Life-Saving Museum's Huggett said that "there were only two paying jobs in Hatteras Island or Pea Island. And that was either with the Life-Saving Service or the Lighthouse Service."

When a ship broke up on the shoals of the Outer Banks, all members of the "checkerboard crews"—comprised of white and black surfmen—worked side by side and day by day and faced the same dangers. But when the storms passed and the patrolmen returned to the regular work of preparing for the next wreck, the African Americans worked as cooks and at other menial jobs, usually serving as the number six or number five man of the crew and almost never rising to the higher ranks.

"The difference between the position of the whites and the African Americans," said Huggett, "was that the African Americans could not get above low-grade surfman. They could be sent but they couldn't transfer on request."

The exception occurred in January 1890 when Richard Etheridge was appointed keeper of Station 17, the first black crew

Rescuers practice on the sandy dunes.

leader in the Life-Saving Service. A native of the Outer Banks, Etheridge had served as a member of the U.S. Colored Troops with the Union Army and later traveled west to finish his term in the service as a "buffalo soldier," according to Arvilla Boswer, who grew up on Roanoke Island and is a descendant of some of the surfmen who worked with Etheridge.

When he returned to North Carolina, he "started working the water again," said Ms. Bowser, fishing and catching turtles as he had done as a youth. He later joined a lifesaving crew at Bodie Island and was finally appointed to the keeper's position at Pea Island by one of the LSS inspectors, Frank Newcomb.

With a Lincolnesque build, a long white beard and a *K* embroidered on his left sleeve to indicate his position as keeper, Etheridge was not only a striking figure but was a humble and strong presence with seemingly instinctive leadership skills. Unlike most former slaves, he knew how to read and write. Wright and Zoby wrote that he "was raised as one of the family" in the home of slave-owner John B. Etheridge.

There is speculation that, since after the Civil War he continued to live with the white Etheridge family until he married in 1867 and because he remained close to John Etheridge's two grown children, he may have been the elder Etheridge's illegitimate son.

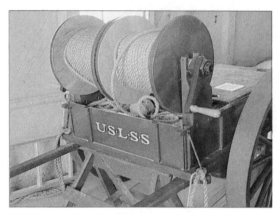

An old rescue wagon

Whatever his paternity, Richard Etheridge knew the sea like few others. He understood the currents and the unforgiving coastline of the Outer Banks. He knew how to sense a storm and how to push himself and his crew to their physical limits. When inspector Newcomb named Etheridge keeper in 1890, he called him "a man among men."

Sent to replace Pea Island's former keeper, who was accused of ignoring distress calls, Etheridge at first commanded a crew of white surfmen. But the whites refused to work for a black man, and Etheridge soon hired his own crew of local African-American fishermen. During his first year in the job, the station was burned to the ground; arson was suspected. Richard Etheridge and his men rebuilt the station the following season.

For the next ten years he led his crew in a steady rhythm of drills and preparation, rescue efforts, and lifesaving maneuvers. Almost every night during that decade, the surfmen patrolled the beaches looking for any signs of ships in trouble. Unable to use lanterns that might confuse sailors into thinking the light came from another vessel, they patrolled the deep sands in almost total darkness, avoiding mounds of driftwood, shards of old ships' hulls, and other beached objects as best they could.

During the storm season and in the winter months, as they trudged along miles of soggy coastline, the driving rains and blowing sand could be blinding. In the hot, semitropical Carolina summers, when the air could be still for days on end and water barely moved in the marshes, the surfmen often were victims of life-sapping diseases such as "the ague"—what the Bankers called malaria. With the only doctor thirty miles away, surfmen did their best to nurse a fevered or injured crew member by using home remedies and island potions until he recovered enough to return to his post—or died.

When a red distress signal went out or a ship was spotted in trouble, the Pea Island crew worked in sync with one another, precisely following Etheridge's orders like well-trained military men. They had to pull and push their heavy beach carts across the dunes, sometimes for miles, before reaching a stranded vessel. Even with the help of mules, the men often had to lean in to the high wooden wheels and push, spoke by spoke, through the sand and surf.

The half-ton wagons carried all the items that were used in rescue attempts of that era. These included picks and shovels, sand anchors, cork life jackets that the crewmen themselves often wore, along with the bulky rubberized "Merriman," an unwieldy kind of nineteenth-century wet suit that was worn in freezing waters.

There was the "faking box," so named because the lifeline was coiled around "fakes" to keep it from becoming tangled before it was shot toward a

A heavy Lyle gun is rolled to the seaside.

ship in distress. The carts also carried Coston flares, a 250-pound Lyle gun (a cannon-like instrument used to shoot the lifeline), X-braces, blankets, a medicine chest, and the "breeches buoy"—a set of pants attached to a floating device that could be sent out along the lifeline and in which a ship's crew could ride back to safety, one by one.

When the surfmen were unable to accomplish rescues with the breeches buoy and other equipment, half the crew might be sent back to the station where a rescue boat was dragged from the boathouse and pulled down the same stretch of beach that the exhausted men had already traveled twice. A deep, wide boat with long, heavy wooden oars, the surfboat was large enough to hold crew and keeper plus the stranded sailors, who would be rowed back to land a few at a time. Depending upon the size of a ship's crew, the rate at which their vessel was coming apart, and the ferocity of wind and waters, the surfmen would sometimes be forced to work for hours, heading time and again into the battering surf to save the last of the ship's survivors.

Bob Huggett and an old rescue wagon

"You nearly always had horrible ocean conditions when you had a wreck," said Bob Hassett. "A nice day, very few ships wrecked . . . a lot of people don't realize that [waves at] the Outer Banks have been recorded as high as ninety feet." And yet Hasset has "records [of] probably eleven ships that were sunk" and the Pea Island team saved everyone on board.

The all-black crew's most famous rescue came six years into Richard Etheridge's tenure. During an October 1896 hurricane, the *E. S. Newman*, a three-masted schooner sailing from Rhode Island to Virginia, was caught in the unrelenting storm and blown off course. Instead of arriving in

Norfolk, the *Newman* was swept onto the shoals at Pea Island, one hundred miles south of its intended destination.

According to reports, the winds were so fierce on October 11 that keeper Etheridge had cancelled Station 17's regular practices and patrols, something that almost never happened. But Theodore Meekins, the surfman who was on one of the fifteen-minute "dogwatches" from the station's crow's nest, spotted a distress flare. Soon afterward, Etheridge and his crew headed south to the site of the wreck. "It was raining so hard they couldn't hardly see," claimed Bob Huggett.

After finally pushing the heavy beach carts through two miles of storm-soaked sand and hurricane-force winds, they reached the section of beach that was just a couple of hundred feet beyond the *Newman*.

Several hours before, the ship's captain, Sylvester Gardiner, had determined that he, his wife, his young son, and the crew were in serious trouble. Their schooner had been battered by the winds for what seemed an eternity and had long since lost most of her sails. Fighting seas that were sometimes as high as thirty feet, the captian often had the ship's wheel spun right out of his hands.

The storm's winds had also reached a nine on the Beaufort scale, a system still used today to determine the strength of storms. (The scale ranges from zero—the calmest—to twelve: "mountainous, hurricane-driven seas that endangered the largest vessels," according to Wright and Zoby.) Although Captain Gardiner had no way of knowing it at the time, a total of four ships would be decimated that day, and he was in one of the worst hurricanes to strike the Atlantic seaboard in fifty years.

Having given up hope that he was near Virginia's Chesapeake Bay, Gardiner feared they were approaching the infamous waters of the Outer Banks. Standing in inches of water at the helm, he knew that the only chance he had of saving the lives onboard was to beach the schooner.

Wright and Zoby said, "Everyone along the coast, surfmen, residents, and fishermen alike, hunkered down and prayed the storm would abate. Meanwhile, the Pea Island crew went out into it."

Bob Huggett called Richard Etheridge and his lifesaving team "men of faith." They must have been uncommonly brave as well, to set out as they did to rescue the terrified souls on the *Newman*. In such weather, most rescue attempts would be all but futile. Yet despite enormous breakers and literally breathtaking winds (possibly as strong as one hundred miles per hour and fierce enough to "damage the anemometer at Kitty Hawk," according to the authors of *Fire on the Beach*), Etheridge and crew pushed ahead in their drenched oilskins until they reached sight of the ship.

Once there, it quickly became obvious that there was no stable sand on which to anchor the Lyle gun that was needed to fire the hawser line on which the breeches buoy could be used. And, even if part of keeper Etheridge's crew could make it back to Pea Island or one of the other stations for a surfboat, it would take them two hours or more to return to the *Newman*. In that amount of time, it would probably be too late.

Although the crew had complete confidence in Richard Etheridge, he would never have taken advantage of their loyalty and ordered them into the seas of that October hurricane. Instead, he asked for volunteers.

His plan was to tie two crewmen together, and, as they fought their way toward the *Newman*, they were to be connected by a lifeline to the five men remaining on the beach. Theodore Meekins, the strongest swimmer of the crew, was the first to say he would go. He was lashed to Stanley "Preacher" Wise, and at first the two men waded forward. But halfway to the ship, the shore gave away beneath them and they began swimming and diving beneath the waves, doing their best to stay clear of the dangerous flotsam that had broken away from the *Newman*.

The first to be taken ashore was the captain's three-year-old son, Tommy. Meekins took off his own cork life vest and put it over the head of the boy. Carrying the child in one arm and protecting his head with the other, and with Preacher as best he could pushing aside the growing pile of lumber and ship's debris in their path, the three moved forward with the rest of the Pea Island crew pulling them to land.

The next to be saved was Tommy's mother. During the course of the next few minutes, the Pea Island team took turns returning to the ship and bringing the remainder of the crew to safety, with the first mate and Captain Gardiner being the last two to leave. Legend has it that Theodore Meekins, the first to volunteer, made every trip.

With all on shore, they wrapped in blankets the most vulnerable—Tommy, Mrs. Gardiner, and one of the elder sailors—and headed back to the station. In one of the fiercest storms of the century, the rescue of the *Newman* had taken less than sixty minutes.

All in all, the Pea Island crews saved more than two hundred lives during the years that the station was in operation—more than any of the other LSS outposts. But it took a hundred years, from the time of rescue of the *E. S. Newman* in 1896, for Richard Etheridge and his men to be honored.

The first step came in 1992 when the United States Coast Guard named a 110-foot cutter the *U.S.C.G.C. Pea Island*, in memory of the all-black crew. Shortly afterward, David Wright and David Zoby, the two graduate students who would later publish *Fire on the Beach*, with the help of Coast Guard Commander Steve Rochon, began the effort to have Etheridge and his crew posthumously awarded the Gold Life-Saving Medal, an award that had been given regularly to white crews of their day.

According to Zoby and Wright, the effort floundered until a fourteen-year-old student, Kate Burkhart, got involved. Burkhart wrote to her state senator, Jesse

Helms, and President Bill Clinton, requesting that the Pea Island crew be so honored. Although the Coast Guard's medals and awards panel had denied a similar request only two years previously, this time the decision makers listened.

Finally, on March 5, 1996, at the Naval Memorial in Washington, D.C., in the presence of descendants of many of the original Pea Island surfmen, keeper Richard Etheridge and his crew—Benjamin Bowser, Lewis Wescott, Dorman Pugh, Theodore Meekins, Stanley Wise, and William Irving—were bestowed the Gold Life-Saving Medal.

As authors Wright and Zoby have correctly written, "A right was wronged, forgotten history recovered."

Chapter 8

Fort Livingston

EVERYONE KNOWS OF A LOCATION THAT SEEMS "SNAKE-BITTEN." NO MATTER what enterprise is attempted there—restaurant, boutique, or office—it always fails. But it's doubtful that any location has ever been more doomed than Grand Terre Island, located about fifty miles south of New Orleans in the Gulf of Mexico.

Grand Terre is one of three barrier islands sometimes collectively called Barataria; the other two are Grand Isle and Cheniere Caminada. Until the first half of the twentieth century, the trio was actually one island large enough to have its own water table, but years of battering storms have reduced the mass to three remnants. And on those slivers of land remain clues to a legendary past.

The city of New Orleans was founded in 1718 and settled by the French and Indians. In 1763 Spain gained control of the city at the signing of the Treaty of Paris, but only thirty-seven years later New Orleans was secretly returned to France. Students of American history will recall that all of Louisiana, including New

Orleans, was sold to the United States in 1803 in a deal negotiated between Thomas Jefferson and Napoleon I—the Louisiana Purchase.

Despite having a population of approximately eight thousand in 1800, New Orleans was in many ways a lawless frontier. French, Spanish, Cajun, and Creole cultures mixed with sailors from around the world to form a roiling melting pot. Pierre and Jean Laffite, two brothers who operated a blacksmith shop, saw entrepreneurial possibilities in the mayhem and started dealing in smuggled goods around 1805.

Strategic location was key to Fort Livingston.

Pirates operated freely from the strategically situated Grand Terre Island that guarded the mouth of the mighty Mississippi River, and ships of any nation were targets for their plundering. By 1810, Jean Laffite had organized these ruffians into a community; he established codes of conduct and managed pirating like a business. He referred to his forces—"a crew of one thousand"—as "privateers" rather than as pirates, and he dubbed himself their captain.

The most lucrative commodity that Laffite's men dealt in was slaves. Although importation of slaves into the United States was banned after 1808, there was still great demand for them throughout the Louisiana Territory, and a strong slave—captured off another ship or purchased in Cuba—could bring as much as $1,200 in New Orleans.

Despite their willingness to attack anyone anywhere, Laffite's men were forbidden, under penalty of death, to raid U.S. ships. Laffite greatly admired the personal freedoms being fostered in the new country . . . and besides, he didn't want to rile the "big new kid."

Laffite lived luxuriously on Barataria, his island enclave named after the mythical land sought by Cervantes's Don Quixote. It was there he built a brick two-story home facing the ocean.

One legendary story tells us a lot about Laffite's clout at the time. A new territorial governor in New Orleans didn't appreciate the influence that Laffite exercised over the area, so he placed a $750 bounty on him. Laffite, not happy about being challenged, placed a $1,500 bounty on the governor. The bounty offer for Laffite was quickly withdrawn.

The War of 1812 didn't reach New Orleans until 1814, only months before the treaty ending the war between the United States and Britain was signed. In early September of 1814, British emissaries visited Laffite on Grand Terre and offered him land, gold, and a commission in the British navy in exchange for information about the American forces and for guides to lead them through the bayou. Laffite promised an answer in two weeks, but he immediately relayed a warning to Governor Claiborne in New Orleans. A week later American ships sailed to Barataria, where they were greeted enthusiastically, but instead of thanking Laffite they destroyed his fleet and captured fifty of his men.

Laffite, who remained loyal to the Americans despite their betrayal, contacted Andrew Jackson and offered him men, flints, and powder. Jackson accepted the offer, and Laffite's men are generally credited with being the deciding factor in the battle of New Orleans, which officially ended the War of 1812. In exchange for their bravery, President James Madison pardoned Laffite and his crew. For the next couple of years, Laffite attempted to regain the ships and property that had been confiscated when the Americans attacked Barataria, but his only success was in acquiring some of them at public auction.

In 1817, Laffite left Barataria and relocated his "business" to Galveston Island off the Texas coast. Only the ruins of his home remained on Grand Terre. Laffite disappeared in 1821 after being forced off Galveston Island by the United States Navy. No one knows how or when he died.

Following the exodus of the pirates, Jean-Baptiste Moussier bought the island and set it up as a sugarcane plantation. Sugarcane farming had been introduced to the New Orleans area in 1751, but seventy years later it remained a very labor intensive, low-margin business. Processing was done by the "Jamaica Train" method—slaves boiled sugarcane in large, open kettles and then separated the cane from the juice. Untold numbers of people were injured transporting the hot syrup from kettle to kettle as the mixture was reduced to sugar crystals. More modern boilers didn't become common until the 1840s, too late to save the Grand Terre operation from financial failure. Once again, the island was abandoned.

After the War of 1812, when British ships were able to move with ease close to the U.S. coast, the U.S. government devised a plan for building forts along the eastern and gulf shorelines to protect against future intrusions. More than two hundred forts were planned, including one for Grand Terre Island because of its strategic location.

Thick walls were filled with sand and shell.

"The fact is that if any country had been able to take over the mouth of the Mississippi River, they could have split the United States in half and we'd probably be speaking another language now," said Michelle Lewis, a ranger with the National Park Service.

On March 10, 1834, the Louisiana legislature ceded the island to the U.S. government and construction began soon thereafter. The new facility was named Fort Livingston in honor of Robert Livingston. As minister to France under President Jefferson, Livingston had negotiated the treaty for the Louisiana Purchase. His distinguished career also included service as a member of the Continental Congress and the committee that formulated the Declaration of Independence. He administered the oath of office to President George Washington in 1789 and aided Robert Fulton in the creation of the first successful steamboat, the *Clermont*, named for Livingston's New York estate.

Work on the fort moved very slowly primarily because of lack of funding and bad weather; the isolation of the island didn't help much either. The foundation of the fort was built on piles of shells that had been left by Native Americans (like the shell-mound islands off the southwest coast of Florida).

"Another interesting thing about the construction of the fort," said Ranger Lewis, "was that while the facade of the fort was built with bricks, the inside—which was sometimes a couple of feet thick—was filled with shells and sand."

The sand and sea have reclaimed the old fort.

Most of the structure was completed by 1849, but despite the fact that New Orleans was the third largest city in the United States by 1852, Fort Livingston was never staffed. A major hurricane in the fall of 1859 caused heavy damage to parts of the vacated fort.

When Louisiana seceded from the Union in 1861, two companies of Confederate volunteers moved into Fort Livingston. Only a year later, however, when Union troops under the command of General David Farragut captured New Orleans, they abandoned the fort without firing a shot.

After the Civil War, entrepreneurs tried again to establish a sugarcane operation and even a shrimp business on Grand Terre, but both failed within a few years. By 1882, even the U.S. government had given up on the island, and General William T. Sherman recommended that Fort Livingston be abandoned.

For the next half century, erosion was responsible for most of the activity around Fort Livingston. In 1880 Grand Terre Island covered about 4,200 acres; by 1932 the island had broken into two pieces; and by 1988 the islands covered only 1,270 acres. Nearly 70 percent of the previous landmass had vanished into the sea.

"People ask, 'Why did Laffite go to this little ratty-looking island?'" said Shea Penland, a University of New Orleans geologist, in a recent Associated Press story. "Well, in 1800 Grand Isle wasn't there. It was just a sand pit with a few trees on it. But Grand Terre was a single island."

The southernmost wall of Fort Livingston washed away in 1965 during Hurricane Betsy, and in 1992 Hurricane Andrew took out a landing strip next to the fort that served researchers working at a marine biology laboratory. In the last decade more than thirty-four million dollars has been spent trying to rebuild dunes and slow down the erosion. But like all things on Grand Terre, these efforts have failed. In spring 2004, the Lyle St. Amant Marine Laboratory, a state fisheries research lab built in the early 1960s, announced that it was leaving Grand Terre. The alternative was to be washed away.

Abandoned for the last time?

Today the remains of Fort Livingston—where no shots were ever fired in war—are bathed by tides, and Grand Terre's colorful past is left bleached a ghostly white under the gulf sun.

Chapter 9

America's Most Haunted City?

SAVANNAH, GEORGIA, HAS ALWAYS BEEN A STRANGE AND UNUSUAL PLACE. Its storied past—from revolutionaries and pirates to the modern-day characters in *Midnight in the Garden of Good and Evil*—has also made it a place often associated with death. It's no wonder that Savannah has been called "one of America's most haunted cities."

James Oglethorpe: City Planner

For a hundred years after English and Spanish explorers first visited the land in the early 1600s, the two colonial powers fought on and off for possession of it . . . barely acknowledging the Creek and Choctaw Native Americans who had lived there for centuries.

The English (even then knowing that possession is nine-tenths of the law) decided that a settlement would enhance their claim to the territory. At about that time, James

Edward Oglethorpe, a benevolent activist who had presided over a British parliamentary committee on prison reform, envisioned a new colony in America where those suffering from poverty and religious persecution could be free. So in what today would be called a "win-win situation," Oglethorpe petitioned King George II for a land grant and a charter for a new colony to be called Georgia (in honor of the king), and the king put him on boat for the New World. Oglethorpe paid his own way.

Oglethorpe's 120 shipmates on the small galley *Anne* were mostly free men, with few if any debtors or prisoners. After three months at sea, on February 12, 1733, they landed at a small bluff overlooking the Savannah River, not far from where City Hall stands today. Later that year a group of Jewish settlers fleeing the Spanish Inquisition joined the settlement, and within a couple of years John and Charles Wesley arrived with a group of Methodists bent on converting the natives.

Before leaving England, Oglethorpe had conceived a plan for the new settlement, effectively making it the first "planned city" in America. Each male settler was given fifty acres—one acre for a town lot, five acres for a garden spot, and forty-four acres for a farm. The town lots were laid out in squares, with residences on the north and south ends and public buildings on the east and west sides. (Twenty-one of Oglethorpe's originally planned twenty-four squares still exist.) The theory was that each square could be defended as an individual fortress, if necessary. Others have suggested that the design of squares had a secondary, occult purpose.

Oglethorpe was a Freemason before coming to Georgia. Only a year after the founding of Savannah, in February 1734, he organized a chapter in his new home and became the first Master of the Lodge. Freemasons are said to have their roots in medieval stonemasons, and consequently architectural symbolism is part of their tradition. The most common symbols associated with Freemasons are the square and compass, tools of the stonemasons' trade. The square is said to represent matter, while the compass represents the spirit. Sometimes a blazing star or an "all-knowing" eye sits atop the square and compass, representing truth.

Those same symbols, of course, had metaphysical references and applications. Occultists perceive great meaning from "square circles." On the other hand, a town laid out in squares creates the appearance of crosses at every intersection, and crosses were said to ward off evil spirits.

Writer Jess C. Henderson summarized the possibilities in an article for *Savannah's Haunting Tours*:

> Perhaps there is more to the city's plan than we know or imagine. By one measurement—using cubits—the original city was a square one thousand cubits on a side. The square is an important pattern in occult lore; a magical square can be used to trace a talisman to achieve a purpose or set a tone or direction for an ongoing enterprise. Could this plan have been, in effect, a magical design of such power and persistence that spirits are trapped between two planes of existence?

Regardless, Savannah was steeped in symbolism from its earliest days.

By 1738, Savannah's eleven hundred settlers were growing restless over General Oglethorpe's strict management. He still opposed slavery and alcoholic drink, and the settlers saw both as necessary for prosperity. Meanwhile, the Spanish continued to threaten the peace from the south. Finally, in 1742, at the battle of Bloody Marsh on St. Simon's Island, Oglethorpe's troops defeated the Spanish for the last time. He lost his battle with the settlers, however; slaves (and rum) were soon coming into Georgia to help farm rice and cotton. The formerly persecuted became the persecutors.

For the next century, Savannah experienced the growth and strife that marked

America's history: revolution against England (1776); capture by the British (the second bloodiest battle of the Revolutionary War in 1778, second only to the battle of Bunker Hill); victory over the British (1782); devastating fires that burned half the city (1796, followed by another in 1820); three deadly outbreaks of yellow fever (one that killed more than seven hundred people in 1820); the Civil War (General Sherman thought Savannah was too pretty to burn, so he gave it to President Lincoln as a Christmas present in 1864); the poverty of Reconstruction; a hurricane that hit between Charleston and Savannah, killing one to two thousand people (1897); and finally the economic growth of the twentieth century. And through it all, Savannah's cemeteries were filled and built over—filled and built over again and again. Native Americans for hundreds of years had buried their dead on Yamacraw Bluff, where Oglethorpe's colonists first landed, and even the first colonial cemetery was full by 1750.

Andrew Nichols, founder of the American Institute of Parapsychology, said, "If I had to name the most haunted city, Savannah would be right up there. Its oldest structures are relatively unchanged and haven't been moved from their original locations. You've had a lot of people living and dying in Savannah."

The Pirates' House dates to 1754.

The Pirates' House

Many of Savannah's ghosts are related to its history as a major port, which brought in sailors, slaves, voodooists, pirates, and traders from around the world. The Pirates' House, built in 1754 and mentioned in Robert Louis

Stevenson's classic book *Treasure Island*, was the scene of many deadly, drunken altercations; and a series of tunnels beneath today's East Broad Street restaurant once ran all the way to the river. Ships' captains in need of hands would grab sotted sailors and drag them through the tunnels to their ships; when the sailors sobered up, they would find themselves at sea. Legend is that a police officer ordered the tunnel openings walled over after he encountered the ghosts of such sailors while inspecting the tunnels.

Steps lead down to the treacherous tunnel.

The 17 Hundred 90 Inn

The 17 Hundred 90 Inn also has a ghost tale related to the sea. Anna Powers, a young, orphaned immigrant from England, came to America looking for a new start in the early 1800s. During her journey, she met and fell in love with a young German sailor named Hans. Some accounts say she became pregnant; others say he broke her heart by courting another; and still others say they were married and he immediately left for sea, never to return.

But all accounts have the same ending: Anna took her life by jumping from the third-floor balcony to the brick courtyard below. Since then her ghost has haunted the inn, primarily around room 204. Many guests and employees through the years have reported strange occurrences—empty chairs rocking, windows opening and closing on their own, footsteps on the empty stairs, and hearing moans and wailing in the night.

Florence: "The Waving Girl"

Savannah's famous "Waving Girl," Florence Martus, is also thought to have been a victim of lost love. When her father was named keeper of the Elba Island lighthouse in 1887, nineteen-year-old Florence moved with him and began waving—a handkerchief by day, a lantern by night—to all ships entering and departing the Savannah port. For the next forty-four years, she claimed she never missed heralding a ship.

The story of "The Waving Girl" spread around the world, and with it spread mystery. Legend says that Florence was waving in tribute to a lost love, always hoping to find him on an incoming ship. She never verified the story or denied it, but it is a fact that she never married. After Florence died in 1943, a bronze statue of her waving was erected on the southern end of Savannah's River Street. People often say they feel "a presence" around the statue.

Habersham House

More than a presence has been felt, and seen, by visitors to the Habersham House (c. 1771), most often referred to affectionately as "The Pink House" because of its rose-colored stucco. James Habersham Sr. was a leading merchant, planter, and public servant during Georgia's colonial era. He collaborated with the Reverend George Whitefield to found Bethesda orphanage. Habersham had three sons—James Jr., Joseph, and John—all of whom sided with the patriots and against their loyalist father in the days before the Revolutionary War. Habersham died in August 1775, just prior to the outbreak of fighting. James Jr. became a successful merchant and politician, and later moved into Habersham House. It was one of the few houses to survive the great fire of 1796 that destroyed more than two hundred Savannah homes.

James Jr.'s younger brothers served heroically in the war; Joseph later became postmaster general of the United States, and John was a member of the Continental Congress. In 1799, at the age of fifty-four, James Jr. reportedly hanged himself in the basement of Habersham House. Today the Olde Pink House is a fine restaurant, but both employees and diners have reported seeing the visage of a well-dressed, middle-aged gentleman passing through the ground-floor halls of Habersham House.

The Hampton Lillibridge House

The most famous haunted house in Savannah is certainly the Hampton Lillibridge house. Built immediately after the great fire of 1796, the Hampton Lillibridge house survived the next great fire of 1820 that destroyed more than 460 buildings. It passed through a variety of owners for the next century and a half, and for a while was operated as a boarding house. During that time a boarder hanged himself in one of the upstairs rooms.

In 1963, wealthy antique dealer Jim Williams purchased the house. Yes, *that* Jim Williams—central figure in the best-selling book and popular movie, *Midnight in the Garden of Good and Evil*. Williams intended to move the Hampton Lillibridge house, and the one beside it, to its present location at 507 East St. Julian Street. But in the process, the second house collapsed and killed a workman. While clearing the old foundation, workers discovered an ancient crypt with eight skeletons inside. Speculation was that the bodies dated back to the yellow fever epidemic of 1820.

After the Hampton Lillibridge house was moved and restoration begun, bizarre things started happening: tools vanished, workers heard eerie noises, and visitors experienced something extraordinary.

"Some folks were walking around the house during the restoration, and they

Hampton Lillibridge: Strange noises within

heard some noises from upstairs," said Robert Edgerly, a longtime Savannah resident. "One of 'em went up to investigate, but when he didn't come back, the others went to check on him. They found him face down at the top of the third-floor stairwell, scared, and just hugging the floor. He said when he got to the top of the stairs, it felt like he'd walked into a pool of cold water, and a force started trying to drag him down the open chimney shaft. That's when he dropped to the floor."

Workers were spooked and restoration virtually stopped. Williams first found a "reader" who told him there were six different ghosts haunting the house. He then found an Episcopal priest who agreed to perform a formal exorcism of the house. In a forty-five minute ritual on December 7, 1963, the Hampton Lillibridge house was cleansed of evil spirits.

A priest performs an exorcism of the house.

"That was the last contemporary exorcism in the United States," said Edgerly. "The house quieted down at first, but Jim said the trouble started again about twelve days later. It wasn't as bad as it was before. The lady that lives there now was going out one evening. She went from room to room turning out all the lights before she left. When she got to her car, she looked back and every light in the house was on. She said she wasn't ever going back in there alone."

Williams later moved into the Mercer house and became well known for his wild parties. It was there on May 2, 1981, that he reputedly shot and killed his sometime associate Danny Hansford. Williams was tried for murder four times in eight years and was ultimately acquitted. He died less than a year later, on January 14, 1990. Although the wild parties have long since ceased, neighbors have reported occasionally hearing music and laughter from the darkened house.

Could it be that Jim Williams has finally met the former residents of the Hampton Lillibridge house?

Chapter 10

Underground Savannah

AS THE OLDEST CITY IN GEORGIA (FOUNDED IN 1733) AND ONE OF THE OLDEST in the South, Savannah has a rich past filled with romance and adventure. But some of the most interesting episodes in its history didn't occur beneath its moss-covered oaks—they took place beneath its cobblestone streets.

An elaborate system of tunnels has existed beneath downtown Savannah for more than two centuries. Many historians believe the British troops first built and used tunnels when they occupied Savannah in the late 1770s. By the time the Continentals surrounded Savannah in the siege of 1782, the British knew they might need a quick, safe passageway out

Many old tunnels have been blocked off.

of the city. The tunnels provided fast access to their boats in the Savannah port.

As soon as the British were driven out, pirates began using the tunnels for a similar purpose—a speedy getaway.

"Pirates would dock their ships down at the river, and go to the Pirates' House—so named for them—to have drinks and tell stories from their adventures all over the world," explained history buff Mitchell Mayer. "When some of the local men would have too much to drink, the pirates would drag them unconscious through the underground tunnels leading back to the dock. They'd wake up the next day on a boat headed for Shanghai, China, or some such place. That's where the phrase 'Shanghaied' comes from, meaning 'taken against your will.'"

The Underground Railroad

First Colored Baptist Church

The maze of tunnels continued to grow during the first half of the nineteenth century as slaves often used them to try to escape. By the time the Civil War started, the "Underground Railroad"—an informal system of safe houses leading from the South to freedom in the North—was already well established.

One of the most popular stops on the "railroad" became First Colored Baptist Church, where the oldest continuous African American Baptist congregation in North America still worships. Built over existing tunnels in 1859 by slaves themselves, who were allowed to work on the project only after their normal daily chores were completed, the church is constructed of bricks made on the riverbank and carried to the building site. The main structure is four bricks thick—built to outlast the slaves' bondage.

Some of the pews in the church are etched with what appear to be abstract symbols, but in fact they are tribal markings by slaves recently brought to America. The markings were a common language among the blacks, tracing family and tribal affiliations.

On the floor of the chapel are thirty-six diamond-shaped patterns formed by bored holes. "They look like diamonds, but that is actually the African symbol for the family," explained Deacon Harry B. James. "And those holes are breathing holes, because there's four feet

The patterns in the floor were actually breathing holes.

of space below this floor where slaves hid until it was safe to move on." No fewer than fourteen tunnels once ran in all directions from beneath the church's floor, some to the river and some to other safe places.

The small space beneath the floors was for hiding.

"Sometimes slaves wishing to escape to freedom came to services in the sanctuary, were given food, and then slipped into the tunnel to hide until it was safe to escape to the river, where they either went upriver by boat or crossed over and hid in barns in South Carolina until their masters stopped looking for them and they made their way to freedom in the North," wrote Bonnie Neely in a recent article. Much planning went into such escape attempts, according to Deacon James:

Slaves couldn't talk to each other openly, so they did it in song. "Steal away, steal away, steal away to Jesus," was really saying, "Slip off tonight; we're gonna have a meeting."And "Swing low, sweet chariot, coming for to carry me home"—now, to the owners, that sounded harmless—they thought we were saying a heavenly chariot was gonna take us to heaven when we died, but we weren't thinking about dying. What that song said is, "The Underground Railroad is coming through, getting ready to carry me home."

A Daring Escape from the Fort

Several miles away on Cockspur Island—little more than a strategically located barrier reef that divides the Savannah River into a north and south channel—stands Fort Pulaski, built between 1831 and 1845 as part of America's "Third System" of shore defense against hostile invaders. The plan stemmed from Britain's attack on Washington, D.C., and Baltimore during the War of 1812. Of more than two hundred forts in the original plan, Fort Pulaski was the last of only thirty that were completed. The fort required eighteen years to complete and consisted of an estimated twenty-five million bricks; its walls were seven and a half feet thick.

Confederate forces took over the lightly staffed fort almost immediately after the start of the Civil War and held it until April 1862, when Union troops won a decisive battle that changed the face of warfare forever. For more than a thousand years such thick-walled fortresses had been considered the best defense against an overwhelming army. But the accuracy and range of newly developed rifled cannons broke through the fortification in less than thirty hours. Confederate forces had no choice except to surrender. For the remainder of the Civil War, rebel prisoners where held at Fort Pulaski . . . except for those who may have escaped in tunnels beneath the fort.

One of Fort Pulaski's strategic tunnels

Powder for weapons was stored underground at the fort, and a series of tunnels connected the storage rooms. It didn't take much imagination to extend some of those tunnels to the outside.

"This place was used to house a group of Confederate officers known as the 'Immortal Six Hundred,'" explained National Park Service ranger Talley Kirkland. "They were retaliatory prisoners that had been selected by the United States government to be particularly mistreated. These men were put on very short rations and were forced to sleep three to a bunk. Late in 1865 a group of seven tried to escape through a tunnel. They swam the moat surrounding the fort and made it to the south channel before they were discovered." There are no records of how many others may have successfully escaped.

Disposal of Bodies

In 1876, when a yellow fever epidemic struck Savannah, the city's tunnel system served yet another purpose.

"A sailor off a ship from Havana got sick and was put in a boarding house, then was transferred to the hospital where he died. That's how the epidemic started," said Paul Henchey. "It began with a high fever, and then the facial features started turning black. Next there was foaming at the mouth, and victims became essentially catatonic. That's why some people originally thought they were possessed and performed exorcisms on them."

More than a thousand people died that dreadful summer. The widespread deaths quickly overran the city's resources. Graves couldn't be dug fast enough and morgues overflowed with bodies, panicking the population and threatening to spread the disease even more quickly.

Doctors at Candler Hospital, the first hospital in Georgia and the second oldest hospital in continuous use in the United States, did what they could to alleviate the panic. They carried the dead into subterranean rooms beneath the hospital—originally used for secretive autopsies, which were illegal—and then smuggled them through tunnels to a park several blocks away.

"When they came out of the tunnels at the park, they'd put the bodies on covered wagons and take 'em down to the river and put 'em on ships," said Paul Bearden. "The ships would take the bodies out into the ocean and dump 'em."

General William T. Sherman slept here.

Marshall House

Tunnels also run underneath the historic Marshall House on Broughton Street. Opened in 1851 as a boarding house, and continuing operations today as a sixty-eight-room luxury hotel, the facility has a storied past.

For example, following his "march to the sea" through Georgia in 1864, General William T. Sherman took up temporary residence in the

Marshall House. The hotel served as a hospital for wounded soldiers until the end of the war.

Seventy years later, the hotel served a merrier clientele. "During the time of prohibition in the 1930s, they operated a speakeasy in the tunnels beneath the hotel," said Bettina Nolin. "Just imagine all the frolicking that must have gone on down there."

So maybe all the ghosts who reportedly inhabit the tunnels under Savannah aren't "trapped" in this world after all. Maybe they're only revelers who don't want the good times to stop.

This tunnel was the site of a former speakeasy.

Chapter 11

What Lurks in the Shadows?

FOR YEARS ADVENTURERS HAVE BEEN TRACKING LEGENDARY MONSTERS BELIEVED to be either genetic freaks or leftovers from an earlier eon. The most famous worldwide are Nessie, the sea creature who reputedly lives in Scotland's Loch Ness, and the Abominable Snowman, known as the Yeti in Tibet, Sasquatch in Canada, and Bigfoot in the American Northwest.

But the South has its own monster legends, and we're not talking about pickup trucks with big tires.

Killer Crawfish

Eating Louisiana Red Swamp crawfish is as old as the region's recorded history. Native Americans harvested and ate the crustaceans—also called crayfish, crawdads, mudbugs, and spiny lobsters—long before the French became Cajuns.

Native Americans baited reeds with deer meat and stuck them in the bayou waters. When they returned later, the reeds would be covered with crawfish.

Mrs. Charles Hebert is generally credited with being the first to put crawfish on a menu in the early 1920s. Soon thereafter they became a staple for poor Cajuns, providing a solid source of protein. *Crawfish étoufée,* the quintessential Cajun dish,

"Killer crawfish" … Eat or be eaten.

didn't appear on menus until the 1950s. Today Louisiana is the largest producer of crawfish in the world with more than sixteen hundred farmers using 111,000 acres of man-made ponds for production.

Many people say crawfish is an acquired taste, but for the omnivorous crawfish themselves, almost everything is tasty. With their sharp claws and endless appetites, they can make short order of any small animal or plant.

Legend says that the Native Americans would take their enemies to the bayou, tie them in water up to their necks, make a couple of small cuts on their legs to induce bleeding, and wait for the crawfish to eat them alive. More than one body has been found eaten away by the ravenous swamp crustaceans, earning them the name of "killer crawfish."

"One day I was out in the swamp in my boat, and I could see swamp crawfish all around the tree trunks," recalled Jim Delahoussaye, a longtime swamper. "An ol' snake came swimming by slowly, and as it did I saw a claw pop out and latch on to the snake's tail. The snake stopped, not thinking much about it, but then another claw latched on to him, and another, and another. Ol' snake started thrashing, and last I saw of him, he was disappearing under the water."

Their "killer" reputation is not limited to Louisiana environs. In parts of Europe and Africa, where Red Swamp crawfish have been introduced—accidentally as specimens or intentionally as a food source—they have devoured and altered entire ecosystems. A single female crawfish can lay one hundred to seven hundred eggs per year, so the aggressive mudbugs soon overtake indigenous plants, eggs, tadpoles, and even small fish.

As one Cajun philosopher said, "The only way to keep them from eating you is to eat them first."

Even water snakes are vulnerable to these crawfish.

Skunk Apes

How can anything that's nearly seven feet tall, weighs five hundred pounds, and is covered from head to toe in long, reddish-brown hair be hard to find? That's what skeptics want to know about the Skunk Apes that reportedly live in the Florida Everglades.

Since Roger Patterson and Robert Gimlin filmed an alleged Bigfoot in the Six Rivers National Forest in northern California in 1967, a number of sightings of similar Bigfoots have been reported across the country. The southernmost sightings have been by Dave Shealy of

© 2001 Loren Coleman and David Darbarkasy

Reputed photo of a skunk ape in Florida

Ochopee, Florida, who claims to operate the world's only Skunk Ape research center.

"The first time I saw a Skunk Ape I was about ten years old," Shealy recalled. "We had a rule in the house that if we could kill a deer before the school bus came, we could stay home and skin it. So my brother and I were out there one morning, and he said, 'What's that over there?' I saw a huge figure like a man or a bear, something like I'd never seen before. My brother yelled, 'Skunk Ape!' and I knew that's what it was. I'd heard about them since I was knee-high."

Shealy said Skunk Apes (he estimated there are a dozen or so living in the Everglades) are not threatening despite their size, but no one has gotten close enough to test that theory. Shealy said their arms come almost to their knees. Aside from their dimensions, Skunk Apes' most distinctive characteristic is their stench, which has

Plaster cast of a skunk ape's foot?

been described as a cross between a skunk and rotten eggs—thus the name Skunk Ape.

"What lots of people don't realize is that the Everglades have underground pockets, underground caverns. Old-timers call 'em 'gator holes,'" said Shealy. "Living under the swamp in those caverns is what makes 'em smell so bad. That's also where they hide out when anyone or anything is looking for 'em."

In 1998, naturalist Jim McMullen—who had spent years tracking Florida panthers—said that he, too, had seen such a creature in the Everglades. "In my opinion, we have an unknown species that needs to be defined," said McMullen.

Dozens of other sightings, plaster casts of footprints, and even some out-of-focus photos have been produced as evidence that Skunk Apes exist but skepticism remains. "In order for us to have one animal out there, there has to be a population," said Florida biologist Larry Richardson. "If there is a population, then we would have roadkill or somebody would have shot one. If that's the case, we would have a specimen, but we don't. On the other side of this coin, if we have an animal so smart that it doesn't get hit by a car or get shot, we need to bring him in and talk him into running for Congress."

Shealy remained convinced that Skunk Apes exist. "There's nothing in this world I would rather do than sit down and have some coffee and crumb cake with a Skunk Ape tomorrow morning," he concluded with a smile.

Lizard Man

In the summer of 1988, in the small town of Bishopville, South Carolina, seventeen-year-old Christopher Davis got the scare of his life.

As he was headed home after working the late shift at McDonald's, Davis's car blew a tire. He stopped on the side of the road next to Scape Ore Swamp to change the flat. When he had finished the job and started to get back into his car, he heard a ruckus in a bean field across the road. Davis described what happened next to the Associated Press:

I looked back and saw something running across the field towards me. It was about twenty-five yards away, and I saw red eyes glowing. I ran into the car, and as I locked it, the thing grabbed the door handle. I could see him from the neck down—three big fingers, long black nails, and green, rough skin. It was strong and angry. I looked in my mirror and saw a blur of green running. I could see his toes and then he jumped on the roof of my car. I thought I heard a grunt and then I could see his fingers through the front windshield, where they curled around on the roof. I sped up and swerved to shake the creature off.

When the terrified teenager arrived home, he woke his father and breathlessly recounted the experience. His father found the mirror on the side of the car door twisted and hanging loose; there were deep scratches and grooves on the roof.

"Something mauled that car," said Sheriff Liston Truesdale. "There was tracks all over the hood. Chrome trim was pulled off and chewed. Whatever it was, was strong."

When the news broke, media from around the world descended on Bishopville.

Lizard Man drew worldwide press attention.

"We had a phone call from England wanting to know if we had an international airport they could fly in to. We probably don't have a hundred houses here," laughed Truesdale. "People from radio stations in Australia would call regular and ask for updates. I loved to hear 'em talk."

Everyone was looking for the seven-foot-tall creature with green scaly skin and red eyes. Posses searched the swamp but failed to find the creature. In the following months, several sightings were reported and numerous three-toed footprints were found, but no hard evidence materialized. By the fall of 1988, the furor had died down.

Sheriff Truesdale kept a poured mold of one of the footprints—a heel, a ball, and three large toes, each one about fourteen inches long and seven inches wide. "If it's really authentic, it's worth its weight in gold," he said. Asked whether he thought the Lizard Man was real or a hoax, Truesdale replied, "I can't prove there was something out there, but I doggone sure can't prove that there wasn't."

Local believers speculated that the Lizard Man hid in the swamp outside Bishopville for about a year, occasionally being spotted by residents. Then in the fall of 1989, Hurricane Hugo—with inland winds of more than 120 miles per hour—blew through the area and altered much of the landscape. Did he die in the storm or move to a more secluded location? Only the Lizard Man knows.

The Altamaha-ha

Darien, Georgia, is a coastal tidewater town located about sixty miles south of Savannah near the mouth of the Altamaha River. Established in 1736 during the colonial period in Georgia, Darien grew to be a major port from which locally grown rice and cotton were shipped to larger ports along the coast.

In the mid-1800s, yellow pine timber from Georgia's interior was rafted down the river to Darien's sawmills and subsequently shipped out. The Civil War disrupted that business, and Yankee forces burned the town of Darien; but by the turn of the century Darien had become an international port as ships from Europe, Asia, and South America docked there for Georgia's prized timber.

When the timber industry died out around 1920 from overcutting, Darien transformed into a commercial fishing village, and today shrimping remains one of the primary occupations in the town of approximately two thousand people.

Carla Jean Mucha and Edward Croff paddle the Altamaha.

The marshy area between Darien and the Atlantic Ocean is eerie and always changing. Dark-water creeks and canals dating from the days of rice farming weave through smooth cordgrass. Twice a day the salty tides cover the marshes, bringing in fresh food for anything living there.

In 1969, two young boys were fishing from their father's houseboat on the Altamaha when something big hit one of the lines. It dove and tugged like a salt-water catfish, and then it ran underwater for an unusual distance.

Could this be the Altamaha-ha or a hoax?

Suddenly a long, dark, eel-like creature broke the surface! At first the boys thought they must have hooked a dolphin, but then they saw a wide, horizontal tail and knew this was something very different. The forty-pound-test line snapped like a spider's strand.

In the years since that first sighting, many fishermen have reported similar experiences. The Altamaha-ha, as the serpent has been named, is said to be from twelve to twenty feet long, about two feet in diameter, and gunmetal gray on top with a creamy underside. Most descriptions suggest a creature that is part eel, part alligator, and part dolphin. It has large, bulging eyes and shark-like teeth; a series of serrated fins run down its spine; it has two front flippers, much like a dolphin's; and its most telltale trait is the flat, spadelike tail that fans out two to three feet.

Despite many sightings since 1969, no one has yet landed an Altamaha-ha, but the marshes around Darien still roil at high tide.

Chapter 12

The Coon Dog Opera

MOST SOUTHERN BOYS GROW UP HEARING TALES ABOUT LEGENDARY WOODSMAN Daniel Boone. A generation even watched him on television as actor Fess Parker starred in the *Daniel Boone* series from 1964 to 1970. But Boone's most recognizable feature—the coonskin cap—was not at all distinctive when he was a boy in Kentucky in the mid-1700s. In fact, it had been common headwear for several hundred years.

Archaeologists believe that raccoons were hunted and trapped by most prehistoric Indian cultures in North America. Raccoon pelts—often used to make caps and coats—certainly were prized by the early trappers and fur traders, and raccoon meat was standard fare on the frontier. Two hundred years later, raccoon fur was still used in the fur industry for collars, cuffs, and hats.

But in recent years, amid protests from animal rights advocates and the manufacturing of artificial furs, the market for raccoon pelts has virtually disappeared. At the same time, food has become as convenient as the corner grocery, so very few people hunt raccoons for cooking anymore. Since raccoons have very few natural predators, the result is that raccoon populations have multiplied as much as 800 percent in the last fifteen years. Today it is not uncommon to see a raccoon in a backyard, sifting through garbage cans or raiding a garden plot—from Canada all the way to Florida.

Coon hunters across the nation—a relatively small but dedicated group—could not be happier. "The toughest part about coon hunting these days is bending over to tie your boots," said Buddy Tanner, an old-school coon hunter from Alabama.

Coon hunting has taken on a ritualistic quality in the South. Generations of rural families have hunted together and have passed on techniques, territories, and dog lines—and for coon hunters, the dog lines are almost as important as the family bloodlines.

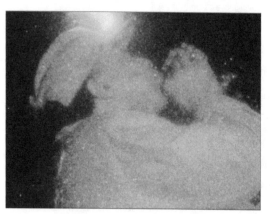

Calling to the dogs during a hunt

"There's a special bond 'tween a hunter and a good coonhound. You learn to communicate with each other. You hear 'em bark and know exactly what they're saying—I got a scent, now I'm on his trail, now I got ol' coon treed. I swear, I know fellers who're closer to their dogs than to their wives," said Tanner.

Six breeds of dogs are used most often for coon hunting: plotts, black and tans, blueticks, redbones, treeing walkers, and English coonhounds. "Almost any dog that will tree squirrels will do," said Bob Rakow, coauthor of *Raccoon Hunting Basics*. "I've owned cow dogs that did the job, a terrier, and even a springer spaniel."

Training a coon dog is similar to training any other hunting dog: familiarize them with the scent (often using a frozen coon) and reward them for successfully tracking and treeing the prey.

Although raccoons are everywhere these days, their favorite haunts are near water and wooded fields. They are omnivorous but prefer acorns, frogs, fish, eggs, corn, and carrion. Raccoons are nocturnal animals; they come down from their den trees at night to feed and play. And that's when the fun begins for hunters.

Following is a colorful description of a hunt, written with the passion common to coon hunters:

A good coonhound is a big, gangling, lop-eared beast. A wag of his bony tail can hurt like a kick in the shin. A good one can cost as much as a horse, and he's always hungry, but his nose and his voice are worth it. He runs with his big muzzle close to the ground, and the news of the night is unerringly telegraphed to his keen brain by a marvelous sense of smell. Once on the trail of a coon, a good hound will never leave it. And his voice has all the full-throated magic of an operatic bass, baritone, or tenor, depending on the dog.

When the hunters reach a chosen spot, a lantern is lit and the dogs let loose. Away they go, fanning out in several directions. The hunters wait, silently, open-mouthed, straining their ears to catch the first sound. Presently a long, hollow moan comes sifting back through the trees and a boy whispers, "There's old Bess." His father growls, "A cold trail. Keep still." A bluetick pup, whimpering and slobbering with excitement, cir-

Other dogs are led into the woods.

cles back into the light cast by the lantern, and then away into the night.

Suddenly, out of the inky darkness and surprisingly near, comes a deep trumpet-like call that booms through the timber. A fat farmer chuckles, "Bugler's on a back trail." Off to the right, a sobbing chop [a short, resonant bark] starts up and settles into a steady bay [a continuous flow of sound]. Finally, in the distance, a sharp commanding bark is heard. The other dogs hush. Again that sharp bark. Someone yells, "Treed!" and everyone dashes off through the underbrush, the lantern bobbing in the mist.

Got ol' raccoon treed and just waiting

When they arrive, panting, the entire pack of hounds is raising a deafening clamor around a big leaning elm. A huge redbone hound leaps upward, clawing and tearing at the bark of the tree. Far up in the elm, two shining greenish eyes reflect the light of the high-held lantern. A brawny young man, arms overhead, struggles through the pack, striking right and left with his leather gauntlets, bawling, "Down! Down!" The coon is treed. The dog opera is over.

Sometimes, if a raccoon is surprised far from his den, such a chase will continue for hours. An old raccoon is wily. He may climb a tree and travel overhead across a patch of timber, by way of the branches, leaving the hounds howling at the foot of the first tree. Or he may gain a long lead by circling, backtracking and confusing his trail by wading in the shallow water of a small stream. He is fairly fast but, if caught on the ground, is a fierce fighter. He is a fine swimmer, utterly at home in water, and has four hands like a monkey. Many a good hound has been drowned by a big raccoon.

—*Nature Bulletin No. 174-A,* January 9, 1965

Forest Preserve District of Cook County, Illinois

Sometimes when a coon is treed, hunters will "harvest" him, that is, shoot him. The pelt can be saved, and the carcass can be left as a reward for the dogs. With the exploding raccoon population these days, thinning them out by hunting is a good thing.

Also, there is a growing risk of raccoon rabies and distemper. Raccoon-strain rabies was first diagnosed in the early 1950s in Georgia and Florida. It was not at that time detected anywhere except in those two states. In 1978, an outbreak of raccoon-

The hunted and the hunter, face to face

strain rabies began in northern Virginia, probably because of the translocation of raccoons by hunters from the Georgia-Florida area. Since 1978, raccoon-strain rabies has spread along the eastern seaboard—from Florida to Maine. Today raccoons are the most frequently reported rabid wildlife species.

"It's a shame that an animal as pretty as the raccoon, with that ringed tail and black mask, is rabid more often than not, while butt-ugly possums are rarely rabid," said a Georgia animal control officer. (Possums do have a high suicide rate, however, as evidenced by their frequently walking in front of cars and trucks.)

Some people (mostly disenchanted wives) think coon hunting is more an excuse for drinking and walking through the woods than an actual sport. But Buddy Tanner disagrees: "Hell, I don't need no excuse for drinking or walking in the woods."

In fact, coon hunting has grown into a multimillion-dollar business. Organized coon-hunting competitions are held throughout the country; *American Cooner* is a monthly magazine with a circulation of more than seventeen thousand; and champion coon dogs can sell for thousands of dollars. The going price for coon pelts may be down, but the coon hunting industry is on the rise.

Chapter 13

Coon Dog Cemetery

THE BOND BETWEEN A HUNTER AND HIS FAVORITE HUNTING DOG IS LEGENDARY. In the process of training, the two become as one—sensing each other's meaning, often responding to only a nod or a wag, working together to track one of nature's wiliest prey. Coarse, macho exteriors can melt away when man and dog are working the woods together.

It is not uncommon, particularly in the South, for good hunting dogs to become involved in custody battles. The callous among us might suggest that taking a man's dog is the ultimate "payback" when a relationship ends.

But even in blissful situations, the loss of a good hunting dog is cause for mourning. Key Underwood lost such a dog—Troop, his incomparable coon dog—on September 4, 1937, in Tuscumbia, Alabama.

Troop, who was half redbone hound and half birdsong, was known throughout the region as the best. He was "cold nosed," meaning he could follow old coon tracks until they grew fresh, and he never left the trail until he had treed the coon.

Troop was the first resident of the cemetery.

When Troop died, Key Underwood decided to bury him in a small, grassy meadow where they often started their hunts. It was a spot where coon hunters frequently gathered to discuss strategies, swap stories, and compare dogs.

Underwood wrapped Troop in a cotton pick sack, buried him three feet down, and marked the grave with a rock from a nearby old chimney.

On the rock, with a hammer and screwdriver he had chiseled out Troop's name and the date.

Other hunters started doing the same when their favorite coon dogs died, and thus began the world's first and only coon dog cemetery, officially known as the "Key Underwood Coon Dog Memorial Graveyard." Today more than 185 coon dogs from all across the United States are buried in this spot in northwest Alabama, about halfway between Red Bay and Tuscumbia, south of Cherokee, in an area today called Freedom Hills. There are elaborate gravestones in the shape of treeing dogs, simple wood-burned markers with heartfelt messages, and everything in between. Today, owners are encouraged to put granite markers on graves.

Later markers became
much more elaborate.

It is said that three requirements must be met before a dog can be buried here:

1. The owner must vouch that the deceased is an authentic coon dog.

2. A witness must declare the same.

3. A member of the local coon-hunters' organization must be allowed to view the coonhound to verify.

"We got stipulations on this thing," said William O. Bolton, the secretary/treasurer of the Tennessee Valley Coon Hunters Association, and caretaker of Coon Dog Cemetery along with his cousin Herbert Henson. "A dog can't run no deer, possum—nothing like that. He's got to be a straight coon dog, and he's got to be full hound. Couldn't be a mixed-up breed dog, a house dog. We wouldn't have nothing if we had every kind of dog out here."

Words of praise honor dogs of yore.

Bolton, eighty years old, has several dogs buried here. He said, "It means a lot to put them out here with top-notch dogs."

Although most markers bear only the dog's name, date of death, and owner's name, many have inscriptions that reflect the affection and pride that the owners felt for their dogs:

"Black Ranger—He was good as the best and better than the rest."

"Will be hard to replace."

"Bragg—The best east of the Mississippi River."

"A joy to hunt with."

"He wasn't the best, but he was the best I ever had."

Coon dog owners may mentally associate their dogs with the best times they can remember. William Bolton described this sensation to a reporter from the *Mobile Register*: "You might have a lot of troubles today, but you could call your buddy up you been coon hunting with, and y'all could get out here in the open. And you'd get away from your troubles and hear them dogs run, and the next day it'd be a lot better for you."

Such comfort deserves a proper burial.

A fittin' restin' place for a coon dog

Chapter 14

The Delta Blues

"I went down to the crossroads
and fell down on my knees,
asked the Lord up above for mercy,
save poor Bob, if you please."

—*from "Cross Road Blues," by Robert Johnson*

ROBERT JOHNSON WAS A SMALL, HANDSOME, ALMOST DELICATE AFRICAN American who lived in Robinsonville, Mississippi, in 1930. In a culture where survival depended on hard work in the cotton fields of the Mississippi delta, those were not such desirable traits.

The teenaged Robert had seen a new breed of minstrels traveling around the South—men who made plaintive sounds on guitars and sang what was being called "the blues"—and realized that those men didn't work in the fields. Maybe "the blues" was his ticket out. He already knew firsthand about the subject matter of the blues—born illegitimate, abandoned by his mother, hardscrabble youth,

Sam Carr has played the blues all his life.

married at eighteen only to have his wife and baby die in childbirth a year later. He just needed a vehicle for expression.

"The Delta Blues is stuff like when you're low in spirits or out of money or out of food," explained musician Sam Carr, son of the legendary bluesman Robert Nighthawk. "When you have the blues, maybe your wife done quit you. Mine should've quit me but she didn't."

Former gospel singer and renowned pastor of Bell Grove Missionary Baptist Church in Clarksdale, Mississippi, since 1975, Willie Morganfield elaborated: "When it comes to the blues, a person sings their feelings . . . what they're going through. It's the same with gospel. If the blues singer's girlfriend leaves him, he says, 'My baby's gone and she won't be back no more.' If that person is a Christian, he'll sing, 'Jesus loves me, this I know.'"

Juke joints are commonplace in the Delta.

Robert Johnson, who had played harmon-
ica most of his life, started going to the local
"juke joints" every night, studying the guitar
moves of men like Son House and Willie
Brown and then practicing on his own.

The Blues House

"Delta Blues was born for the most part in
juke joints," explained Edward Komara,
director of the Blues Archive of the
University of Mississippi in Oxford. "These
tended to be small, one-room structures near places where people lived and worked
in the cotton fields. The music generally lasted as long as the beer held out."

Johnson spent plenty of time in his "classrooms"—the juke joints—taking in
everything he could. But competence came slowly. Son House recalled in an interview for the magazine *Living Blues* how, during breaks, young Johnson sometimes
would pick up one of their guitars and begin playing:

And such a racket you never heard! It'd make the people mad, you know. They'd
come out and say, "Why don't y'all go in and get that guitar away from that boy!
He's running people crazy with it!" I'd come back in, and I'd scold him about it.
"Don't do that, Robert. You drive the people nuts. You can't play nothing."

Johnson spent the next year moving around the Delta, playing the joints and in
work camps for the men building levees and roads through-out the region. He saw
all the great musicians performing the new music—Charlie Patton, Robert
Nighthawk, Sonny Boy Williamson, Elmore James, Howlin' Wolf, and Hacksaw Harney,
among others—and learned and borrowed from each of them.

The next time Son House saw Robert Johnson perform, he was dumbstruck. The boy who couldn't "play nothing" had become a masterful blues guitarist. How had he improved so much so quickly?

"The rumor was that Johnson may have sold his soul to the devil, 'cause he was remembered as not being a very good guitar player and then coming back a year later as an amazing one," said Komara. "The legend was that if you wanted to improve your guitar skills, you would take your guitar and go to where two country roads intersected. Then you'd wait until midnight, and supposedly a seven-foot-tall man, or sometimes the devil himself, would come out. You'd give him your guitar, he'd retune it, and you were automatically blessed—or cursed—with amazing guitar skills."

Deals with devil occur at the crossroads.

The notion of dealing with the devil at the crossroads was part of African folklore brought to America by slaves. Delta Haze Corporation, which represents the estate of Robert Johnson, explained:

The deity Esu was believed to be the guardian of the crossroads, and was an intermediate between gods and humans. When Christianity was brought to African culture, these pagan gods were labeled as being similar to the devil. Hence, the concept that one could find the devil at a crossroad.

Mae Smith of the Delta Blues Museum in Clarksdale, Mississippi, said Johnson fueled the rumor:

When he came back after that year away, he was so good that everyone said he must have sold his soul to the devil. He never would deny it, so the rumor just got bigger and bigger. Now it's a phenomenon. People come here from all over the world wanting to know where to find the crossroads.

The rumor was advanced even further by a physical peculiarity. "Robert Johnson's right eye bulged more than his left," said Komara. "A lot of people thought that was a mark of his deal with the devil."

A less dramatic explanation for Johnson's improvement is that he was tutored and practiced hard. When he left Robinsonville, Johnson moved to Hazlehurst and secretly married Callie Craft, a woman at least a decade older than he was. She doted on Robert and encouraged his new friendship with Ike Zinnerman, an excellent blues guitarist. For the next year, Johnson was like Zinnerman's shadow, hanging out and learning everything he could from the mentor. Friends said he practiced around the clock, often in the woods by himself, and performed at every opportunity to improve his skills. By the time Robert Johnson returned to Robinsonville, his talent was undeniable. But once he made that point, it was time to move on again . . . without Callie.

Johnson played levee camps, coal yards, and juke joints all across Mississippi and into Arkansas. As his reputation grew, so did his audiences and overtures from "the ladies," for whom Robert always made time. He even traveled with other musicians to Chicago, Detroit, and St. Louis to play the blues.

By the middle 1930s, Johnson wanted to make a record, as his old friends Willie Brown, Son House, and Charlie Patton had done. He contacted the local salesman for the American Record Company, who was also a talent scout, and earned an audition. Johnson's first recording session came in November 1936 in San Antonio, Texas, and

Playing the Blues

included the song for which he is best known, "Terraplane Blues." His second and last session was held in Dallas in June 1937. The two sessions generated forty-two tracks, of which thirteen were alternate versions. Johnson was paid a modest fee but received no royalties.

A year later, in July 1938, Robert returned to Robinsonville as part of a Mississippi tour with Sonny Boy Williamson. As he was prone to do, he made friends with the local ladies, including the wife of one juke joint's owner. Late one evening during a break, somebody handed Robert an open bottle of whiskey. Although Williamson tried to discourage him from drinking from the opened bottle, Johnson drank it anyway. Within hours he was violently ill, and two days later—August 16, 1938—he died at the age of twenty-seven. The doctor said he died of strychnine poisoning that was probably administered through the whiskey in the opened bottle. Jealousy had extinguished one of the brightest stars in blues music.

Thanks to the Texas recording sessions, Johnson's reputation has held up well through the years. He is credited with inspiring such blues legends as Elmore James and Muddy Waters, who helped create the Chicago style of electric blues in the 1950s. And that style, of course, was part of the foundation on which rock 'n' roll was built. Modern guitar superstars like Keith Richards and Eric Clapton have cited Johnson as an early influence on their styles.

Not bad for a man who was told: "Don't do that, Robert. You drive the people nuts. You can't play nothing."

Chapter 15

The Fort Fisher Hermit

BY MANY MEASURES, ROBERT HARRILL WAS "TURNED FUNNY." HE WAS UNABLE to hold a job, was a failure as a family man, heard "voices" and was committed to a mental hospital, and finally forsook convention and modernity to move into an abandoned bunker on a North Carolina beach where he lived off seafood and berries. Yet in one year, approximately seventeen thousand people visited him seeking wisdom—or maybe they were just curious.

Harrill was born in February of 1893, probably in Shelby, North Carolina, although some reports say South Carolina. According to Michael Edwards, author of four books on Harrill and the undisputed expert on the subject, his mother and two brothers died of

Robert Harrill, pre Hermit

typhoid fever when Robert was young. His father remarried a woman that Robert did not like, and apparently the feeling was mutual, for he told many people that she made his childhood miserable. Years later he proposed writing a book titled *A Tyrant in Every Home*—a direct reference to his stepmother.

To escape his unpleasant home life, Robert spent a lot of time alone roaming the woods and fields around his home. He reportedly felt great comfort being close to nature.

Regular work didn't work for Harrill.

After graduating from high school, Robert studied to become a Baptist minister, but that pursuit failed. He tried farming, the textile mills, and even sales, but nothing seemed to fit. In 1913, Robert, at the age of twenty, married Katie Hamrick and tried to fashion a "normal" life, but once again conformity eluded him. Katie eventually took the children and moved to Pennsylvania. Shortly thereafter, Robert—who had admitted to hearing for much of his life "voices in my head, telling me how bad I was"—was committed to a state hospital.

While in the hospital, Robert discovered the writings of Dr. William Marcus Taylor, who taught and lectured on biopsychology—the belief that the body and mind are inseparable, and that what affects one also affects the other. After he was released from the hospital, Robert attended a lecture by Dr. Taylor and began a long student-pupil relationship with him. Taylor encouraged Robert to seek his "true self," to rid himself of his troubled past, and to concentrate on a new, positive future.

In the summer of 1955, at age sixty-two, Harrill took the first step toward self-discovery. With only a suitcase full of possessions, he left Shelby and hitchhiked to Fort Fisher, North Carolina, south of Wilmington, to a beach he remembered fondly from an earlier vacation. But almost before he could shed his coat, much less his unfortunate past, local authorities charged him with vagrancy and threatened to put him in jail. Michael Edwards reported that "the sheriff later 'assisted' him back to Shelby."

A year later, more resolved than ever, Harrill returned to Fort Fisher and moved into a deserted World War Two–era bunker in the salt marsh barely out of the ocean's reach. The bunker, which probably had been used to store antiaircraft munitions, was approximately nine feet by fifteen feet with an eight-foot ceiling. The only light came from an entry doorway and a small ventilation slit in the back wall. The walls were made of solid concrete a foot thick.

The stark bunker was all the home he wanted.

The bunker provided adequate shelter from the elements, and seafood and berries provided basic nourishment.

Harrill was determined to avoid the accoutrements of normal life, to get rid of the ties that bound him, and to coexist with nature as much as possible. He let his hair and beard grow long. He planted a garden and grew seasonal vegetables in his seaside "Eden." On occasion, however, nature was not a welcoming host: mosquitoes, brutal

The Hermit in his element

heat, hurricanes, and winter weather often made his life difficult. But not as difficult as people sometimes made his life.

Harrill was harassed by local teenagers, and many of his "neighbors" did not like having a strange man live on a public beach. Once again, Harrill was threatened with

Harrill trapped raccoons for food and fellowship.

vagrancy charges, but eventually his courtroom logic paid off—if he was a vagrant for spending his days and nights on the beach, so were thousands of tourists who did the same all summer. The judge agreed.

By the mid-1960s, word had spread about this intentional Robinson Crusoe. But instead of criticism from traditionalists, Harrill began getting praise from the rising "hippie" population. They, like he did, sought distance from "the establishment," and advocated peace and tolerance and a revitalized respect for nature. Harrill became known as "the Fort Fisher hermit" and gained almost mythic status with this new generation.

"Robert was talk radio before talk radio," said Edwards. "People enjoyed hearing his rants against crooked politicians and crooked law enforcement officers and the evils of modern society." They also started leaving cash contributions, which were not refused.

When asked why he attracted so many people, Harrill told Edwards, "Everyone has the desire from time to time to be a hermit, to be alone, to relax and perhaps converse with their maker. It's much easier to wish yourself a hermit than to be one . . . I represented the hermit in them—that's why I'm so successful."

After a lifelong search, Robert Harrill had apparently found meaning and purpose in his life. He had become a role model rather than one to be ostracized. This little man, barely five and a half feet tall, had become almost bigger than life.

Tourists often had their pictures made with the Hermit.

"I'll never forget shaking hands with him," said local resident Leslie Samuel Bright. "It was like holding an eagle's talon—scaly, hard, with fingernails a quarter inch thick."

On June 3, 1972, at age seventy-nine, Robert Harrill was discovered dead in his bunker. Like most of his life, his death had a tinge of mystery. Official cause of death was listed as a heart attack, but some people suspected more.

"My understanding is that people came out that night to harass the hermit," said biographer Edwards. "He was alone in the bunker, and they drug him in his sleeping bag over toward the marsh. There was a struggle and one of them lost a shoe,

A proper epitaph for Robert Harrill, the Fort Fisher Hermit

which was left in the mud. In the course of the melee, Robert had a heart attack. They dragged him back to the bunker, threw him inside, and took off."

Another theory is that Robert was killed in a robbery attempt. In fact, more than one thousand dollars was found buried in and around the bunker.

Harrill was buried in Shelby, but in 1988 his body was exhumed and reburied near Fort Fisher. His grave marker identifies him as the "Fort Fisher Hermit," and the inscription says, "He made people think."

In Robert Harrill's mind, that was a worthwhile pursuit for a man.

Chapter 16

The Town(s) Sherman Didn't Burn

THERE IS THAT OPENING SCENE FROM *GONE WITH THE WIND* WHERE NEIGHboring plantation owners gather for a barbecue and Scarlett and the other dewy young women, in their huge, billowy hoop skirts, move among the adoring men as if they are floating inside clouds of meringue; it is the kind of party where the guests came from all over the county and where the food and fun lasted for days. On the other end of the spectrum is the scene from David O. Selznick's movie version of Margaret Mitchell's Civil War epic where it looks as if not only Atlanta is burning but all the world is aflame. Those two set pieces have become emblazoned on the minds of southerners for decades and left us wondering if at least two images we have of the era are correct: Was there a party mentality among the white gentry before the war and, after the war began, was a wick lighted in Atlanta that stretched searing all the way to the sea?

Well, yes and no, apparently. Madison, Georgia, is situated sixty miles east of Atlanta on what would have been that burning wick to the Atlantic but is now called Interstate 20. Named by the state legislature in 1809 for James Madison, the newly elected president at the time, Madison became the county seat.

The historic courthouse in Madison, Georgia

Today it boasts historical buildings and antebellum homes that draw thousands of tourists annually to its Chamber Music Festival, the May Tour of Homes, arts and antiques shows, and the Morgan County African American Museum. Movie crews come regularly to film its streets and town square and structures such as the 1842 Presbyterian Church where Woodrow Wilson married his first wife, a local woman named Ellen Axson, and the Church of the Advent, which was built in the 1840s for the Methodists and whose original slave gallery now houses the Episcopal church's organ.

But it is Madison's homes, with their expansive porches, fluted columns, window etchings, and sweeping lawns that are the biggest attractions in town. Homes such as the Greek Revival Baldwin-Ruffin-Lanier House (the original building of the Baptist's former Georgia Female College); the Barnett Parish House (which is thought to have been constructed for the rival Madison Female Institute, a Methodist women's college); Dovecoat House (circa 1830); the 1810 Stagecoach House; and the Stokes-McHenry House on Old Post Road, which has been occupied by members of the same family for seven generations.

Many of those homes were built as town homes for well-to-do planters who lived in north central Georgia. Unlike the thousand-plus-acre plantations in the lower two-thirds of the state and in other areas of the Deep South, the planters in

Georgia's Piedmont country grew pine trees and lived off two hundred- to five hundred-acre "garden farms," says Bette Copelan in Madison's Welcome Center. Madison was founded in part because these planters wanted a convenient place where they could gather at the end of the work week and entertain friends in elegance. While they resided in the country during the week, they headed to their town homes in Madison from Friday to Sunday, where, as Ms. Copelan claims, they "partied" through the weekend.

Antebellum homes still line Madison's streets.

Legends abound as to why their homes were spared by Union soldiers. A sidewalk poll may give such answers as the town's delicious fried chicken. Or the lovely Madison ladies. Or that the city was too beautiful to be burned. Or, as it is rumored in many small southern cities that still have antebellum buildings, some in Madison believe that Sherman had a local girlfriend to whom he made the promise of sparing her town.

Marguerite Copelan

The "girlfriend" seems to be the most popular story, according to Bette Copelan's daughter, Marguerite, who is the Executive Director of Madison's Convention and Visitors Bureau. But the truth is, Ms. Copelan says, William Tecumseh Sherman never set foot in Madison. And if he did indeed spare the town as a favor, it may have been for a Union-supporting Georgia congressman instead of a Madison belle.

The story goes that Joshua Hill had befriended Sherman's brother at West Point. He was later elected to congress, but he resigned in 1861 when he refused to join his fellow Georgians in seceding from the Union. Although known in the area as a Unionist, Hill supposedly redeemed himself among the Confederates when he led a small delegation of townsmen to Atlanta to ask the Union General—who was reported to be burning his way to Savannah—to bypass Madison.

Marshall "Woody" Williams has lived in Madison for fifty-two years and has been the town's official, full-time, unpaid Archivist for nearly twenty. His office on Hancock Street behind the Morgan County Court House is housed in the former county jail; the red brick building, with its high-pitched roof and bars on the second floor windows, is named in his honor. There's a sign on the building's fortified metal door that reads: "Researchers Enter Here. Push Door to Open. If it opens, Archivist is in. No need to knock."

Williams says that there "might be truth" to some of the tales of the Madison's Civil War days, but "I only vouch for what I've found." What he has found is that Joshua Hill rode out to meet not with Sherman but with one of Sherman's generals, the Left Wing commander Henry Slocum. When Hill met Slocum, according to Williams, it was to claim the body of his [Hill's] son instead of asking for mercy for Madison's buildings.

"I've been looking for this burning business" and looking for evidence that Joshua Hill met with Sherman for fifty years, says Marshall Williams. Although there are stories that Sherman mentions the meeting in his memoirs, Marshall Williams has never found it. The "biggest tale," according to Williams, was Joshua Hill's preventing the razing of the city by Slocum's army in November of 1864. Instead, it was most likely General George Stoneman's calvary that did the most damage to Madison by "pretty well emptying the stores of their goods," says Williams. George Stoneman had been Stonewall Jackson's roommate at West Point, held the distinction of being the highest ranking officer to ever be captured by the Confederacy during the war, and later was elected Governor of California. When he entered Madison in the summer of 1864, he was said to have been suffering mightily from an almost debilitating case of the hemorrhoids. Whether that condition affected his disposition is unknown, but Stoneman ordered his troops to ransack the town's businesses, and he instructed local slaves to help themselves to what lay on the streets. Anything that remained was burned. But it was only the merchandise that was destroyed, Williams points out, not the buildings. All of this occurred several months before Slocum's forces even came to town.

Still, despite Williams' findings, Joshua Hill is credited with saving Madison and its historic buildings. His own home was built in 1835 and sits on a lot that takes up an entire block between Old Post Road and Academy Street. With its Doric columns, double front doors, and second story bal-

cony, it is a classic example of the architecture that was completed between 1830 and 1860 in Madison and other small Southern cities. Today, a park on South Main is named in Hill's honor and the once anti-secessionist has become a favored son.

Like so many of the myths having to do with the Civil War and especially with the Union's infamous General Sherman,

Joshua Hill's stately home, built in 1835

Madison was far from being the only town that was saved. In fact, most of the towns in the path of the Union Army's march to Savannah, along what has become known as Georgia's Antebellum Trail, were spared. According to Marshall Williams and Dr. Edward J. Cashin, an historian living in Augusta and the author of numerous books including *General Sherman's Girl Friend,* very few Southern cities were torched. Aside from Atlanta and Columbia, the only other town burned in Georgia was Griswoldville, a now-extinct and little known place northeast of Macon where a pistol factory was located. Instead of razing entire towns, what happened most often was similar to what occurred in Madison: stores were depleted of goods and the depots and cotton gins were burned. But the homes and businesses were left intact and the towns as a whole—including Athens, Rutledge, Covington, Macon, Augusta, and even the state capital at the time, Milledgeville—were spared.

Still, the legends remain and, according to Elissa R. Henken, a University of Georgia folklorist, "Each town treats itself as the one and only one that was saved."

That burning wick seems almost as much legend as Sherman's numerous loves and the illegitimate children some claim are buried around the South. In truth, General Sherman spent the majority of his evenings poring over maps of the land that would be traversed the next day, causing his troops to think him prescient. If there was any partying going on in the middle of the nineteenth century, it was done by the planters in their elegant town homes before the war, not by Old Will between battles.

Richard McMurry, author of *Atlanta 1864: Last Chance for the Confederacy* and one of the country's leading Civil War experts, says that many of the legends about Sherman burning half the South were generated by Sherman himself. "If he conveys that myth to the Confederate soldiers, he really undermines their will to fight. Sherman's bark was a lot worse than his bite."

Another historian, Anne J. Bailey, author of *War and Ruin: William T. Sherman and the Savannah Campaign,* agrees: "If [Sherman] had told his men to lay waste to the land, they could have done a lot worse than they did."

However, lest you begin to think that Sherman did no ill, be sure to read what comes next about the unfortunate women of Roswell, Georgia.

Chapter 17

Roswell Women

TENS OF THOUSANDS OF PEOPLE EVERY DAY DRIVE UP AND DOWN ONE OF THE main arteries and busiest streets in Atlanta, Georgia—passing apartment complexes, strip malls, churches, car washes, grocery stores, gas stations, quick stops, automobile dealerships, and samples of just about every fast-food chain in America. This road originates at its intersection with Peachtree Road in the heart of Buckhead, Atlanta's best-known suburb and one of the most affluent communities in the nation. Buckhead was named for the buck's head that settler Henry Irby purportedly mounted in front of his general store and tavern in the 1830s.

From this intersection, Roswell Road leads north and rises in elevation until it reaches the town square of the small historic city of Roswell. Drivers dart in and out of traffic all along the approximately fifteen miles of asphalt from Buckhead to Roswell, dodging the road's ubiquitous potholes and changing lanes with nerve-wracking frequency. Through traffic light after traffic light, they speed northward with little or no knowledge of the dramatic history that transpired nearby: how the land was taken from Native Americans and sold to the city's namesake, the slaves who labored there for the benefit of the wealthy, and the hundreds of women whose lives were forever changed there during the Civil War.

When Roswell King purchased large tracts of land in north Georgia in the late 1830s and started a new career manufacturing textiles, he was already a successful businessman in his seventies. A native New Englander, King had been born in Connecticut in 1765. He became skilled in construction, and that talent led him to the prominent southern port of Darien, Georgia, in the late 1700s. King began using tabby (a regional cement-like material made of sand, lime, and oyster shells) to help build homes such as the Sapelo Island mansion of Thomas Spalding, one of the wealthiest planters in the state.

With Darien as his base, King served as a commission broker for the local commodities—rice, cotton, and lumber. He held various other key positions in the area, including justice of the peace, surveyor, lieutenant in the local militia, and member of the Georgia House of Representatives. It was his job overseeing the enormous holdings of an absentee plantation owner, however, that sealed King's reputation in the region.

In 1802, King became the estate manager for Major Pierce Butler, a wealthy planter who lived in Philadelphia. The Irish-born Butler had immigrated to American in 1767 as a major in the British army. A self-made man and a resolute Federalist who was elected twice to the U.S. Senate, Butler married Mary Middleton, the daughter of a prominent South Carolina plantation owner.

In the late 1700s, determined to create his own wealth and a name for himself,

Butler developed immense estates on Georgia's St. Simons Island at Hampton Point and nearby Butler's Island. On these remote holdings in the Altamaha River estuary, with more than five hundred slaves planting hundreds of acres in rice and sea-island cotton, King made his fortune. Slavery, which had been legal in the colonies since 1749, was challenged at the 1787 Constitutional Convention in Philadelphia, where Pierce Butler was a delegate. He was one of the representatives who argued successfully for its continuation.

Butler, however, preferred the more comfortable and luxurious life in his homes in Pennsylvania to the day-to-day responsibilities of overseeing two vast plantations on Georgia's barrier islands, so he turned over the management of his southern empire to the forceful and efficient Roswell King in 1802. King and one of his sons soon earned reputations as hard-fisted managers of the Butler family plantations in McIntosh and Glynn counties along the state's coastline, where 80 percent of the population was comprised of slaves. As production increased and the plantations became increasingly efficient and lucrative, Butler delegated more and more of the decisions and responsibilities to King. But as profits grew, so did the tension between the two men.

Pierce Butler was known in the region for treating his slaves with relative decency and demanding that they were adequately housed, clothed, and fed. King, however, was a severe taskmaster and disciplinarian and was known for driving the slaves with little mercy. A final falling out came when nearly a fifth of the Butler slaves ran off with British forces and sailed to Bermuda. Butler blamed his overseer for the slaves' departures and the subsequent financial loss to his plantation. In 1820, Roswell King resigned his position and for the next decade worked as a director for the Bank of Darien.

The relationship between the two families continued, however, as King's son,

Roswell Jr., took over the administration of the Butler plantations. The younger King remained in that position for nearly twenty more years until 1838, when Butler's grandson moved temporarily to the family's estates on the Sea Islands.

Fanny Kemble was one of the most beautiful and beloved actresses of the British stage in the nineteenth century. Born into an acting family in 1809, she made her London debut at twenty years of age playing the female lead in "Romeo and Juliet." She soon became an international celebrity. On a tour of the southeastern seaboard in the early 1830s, she met, fell in love with, and married Pierce Butler's grandson.

The beautiful Fanny Kemble

Son of the elder Butler's daughter Sarah and her husband, James Mease, this grandson was originally named Pierce Butler Mease. But following a stipulation in his grandfather's will, the younger Pierce changed his name to Pierce Mease Butler. He and his brother John (who also changed his surname to Butler) became the major heirs to the old man's estates on the Georgia islands. There they continued to plant cotton and rice and, much like their grandfather, served mainly as absentee owners with Roswell King's son handling the daily management of the plantations.

Unlike the Butler family patriarch, however, the younger Pierce Butler lacked business acumen, and years later he was forced to sell 429 men, women, and children to avoid insolvency. It was, according to the New Georgia Encyclopedia, "the largest sale of human beings in the history of the United States."

From the beginning of her marriage to Pierce Mease Butler, Fanny Kemble was emphatically opposed to slavery, but her vocal opposition was mainly philosophical. When the couple and their two young daughters finally traveled to the Georgia coast in the winter of 1838, the plantation society that she observed firsthand appalled her. Their stay of several months on St. Simons and Butler's Islands was a life-altering experience for the family and ended up cutting a fatal chasm in the couple's marriage.

During that winter in Georgia, Fanny Kemble kept detailed accounts of the people she saw and the experiences she witnessed, chronicling in particular the moving stories of slave women. Originally written as a series of thirty-one letters to her friend Elizabeth Dwight Sedgwick in Massachusetts, the correspondence was never mailed. It wasn't until nearly three decades later, after the outbreak of the Civil War, that the letters were made public. Kemble finally decided to publish the letters in 1863, because of her growing concern over pro-slavery sympathizers in England.

Long since divorced from Pierce Butler, her eyewitness account of despotic overseers, indifferent landowners, and the poignant lives of slaves, entitled "Journal of a Residence of a Georgia Plantation in 1838 – 1839," caused a sensation both in England and in the United States. The majority of British readers were revolted by the depiction of slavery, while equal percentages of southern Americans disputed it.

During the years that Roswell King worked for the Bank of Darien, gold was discovered in north Georgia, especially in the small Appalachian towns of Dahlonega and Auraria. On a scouting trip for the bank, King traveled north on horseback to an area where the "river of painted rocks"—the Chattahoochee River—merged with Vickery Creek. The Cherokees called the rich, thick forests and flowing waters enchanted land. King called it opportunity.

It was at this time that the state of Georgia declared the Cherokee Nation "illegal." While the Cherokees tried desperately to protect their rights, President Andrew Jackson ignored a U.S. Supreme Court ruling and, in the late 1830s, called for the removal of the Cherokees from their native lands and sent them on the forced march westward now known as the Trail of Tears.

The land that was seized from the Cherokees was divided into counties and dispersed to white settlers in land lotteries. Roswell King purchased the land that would become known as Roswell from one of these lottery winners. Two of King's sons joined him in north Georgia, and with the help of numerous slaves, they began building a well-planned city that included large homes, a church, cotton mills, and housing for the mill workers.

King's entrepreneurial skills and an abundant supply of local cotton led to the success of the Roswell Manufacturing Company, soon the largest mill in north Georgia. Roswell King and his sons persuaded other planters from the coast to join them by offering sixteen-acre plots of land and stakes in their manufacturing enterprises. King and his family and friends prospered as the mills received constant orders for yarn, cloth, rope, tenting, and other materials.

James Stephens Bulloch, one of the prominent plantation owners from the coast, soon became a business partner with Roswell King. With the help of slave labor, Bulloch built Bulloch Hall, a Greek Revival mansion, near the town square. Major Bulloch's daughter Martha ("Mittie") married Theodore R. Roosevelt Sr., a member of the "Oyster Bay Roosevelts," in the dining room at Bulloch Hall and subsequently became the mother of the twenty-sixth president of the United States, Teddy Roosevelt. Mittie was also the grandmother of Eleanor, who married Franklin of the "Hyde Park Roosevelts" and became America's First Lady during the years leading up to World War II.

In 1844, Roswell King died and was buried in the town's new cemetery. But the mills he and his sons had founded continued to flourish, and Roswell became one of the most important manufacturing towns in the region. Its mills were still running strong by the time of Georgia's secession from the Union in January 1861, and soon began producing "Roswell Gray," the cloth used to make Confederate uniforms.

Although at the start of the Civil War the majority of well-to-do Roswell families fled to safety, the mills continued to operate until the summer of 1864, when Brigadier General Kenner Garrard arrived with the Union cavalry and thirty-six thousand troops occupied the city.

As the Union forces approached, the owners turned over their mills to Theophile Roche, a French overseer. In a desperate measure to try to save the operations, Roche flew a French flag. The attempt was initially successful as a

Remains of one of the historic Roswell mills

captain in the Seventh Pennsylvania Calvary allowed the people to continue to work. Michael Hitt, a historian and the author of *Charged with Treason*, wrote:

And they did [work] for a full day with an entire regiment of Union Cavalry around them. When he [the captain] arrives the next day, he pulls an inspection at the mill. French flag's still flying. People are still working. And he noticed they were weaving a very fine gray cloth with the capitalized letters "CSA."

The letters stood for Confederate States of America, and the officer realized that the supposedly neutral French flag was a hoax. When he reported the events to Gen.

William T. Sherman, the Union leader ordered the mill destroyed and its workers charged with treason.

"I repeat my orders that you arrest all people, male and female, connected with those factories, no matter what the clamor," said Sherman, "and let them foot it, under guard, to Marietta, when I will send them by [railroad] cars to the North." Since the majority of the local men were fighting in the rebel army, it was mostly women who had been employed at the mills. Between four hundred and five hundred women and their children were initially held prisoners at the Georgia Military Institute in Marietta. From there they were given a few days' rations and loaded onto boxcars heading north, mostly to Kentucky and Indiana. Over the years a few of the women, such as seamstress Adeline Bagley Buice, made their way back to Georgia. But even Buice's story is a tragedy: pregnant at the time she was charged with treason and deported, it took five years for her young daughter and her to make it back to Roswell from Chicago on foot. By the time she reached her home, her Confederate husband, thinking she had died during the war, had remarried.

Reenactment of Sherman's March

The majority of the Roswell women, with little means of supporting themselves and with little hope of returning to Georgia, stayed where they had been deported and began to marry. Although there were cries of outrage and disbelief in both the Northern and Southern presses in the summer of 1864, there was still a war raging and the unfortunate women and their fates were mostly forgotten.

Georgia historian Webb Garrison, in his book *Atlanta and the War*, said: "Had the Roswell incident not been followed immediately by major military developments, it might have made a lasting impact upon opinion. In this century [the twentieth], few analysts have given it the emphasis it deserves."

"At the end of the war nobody stepped forward and brought these people back where they belonged," said George Thurmond, who spearheaded a movement to build a monument near the Roswell Mill in honor of the displaced mill workers. "Nobody really knows what happened to them, and that's one of the reasons why we decided it was important to have a monument here in their memory."

The monument was commemorated in a special ceremony in July 2000. It has a broken column representative of, according to Thurmond, "the shattered lives of the women and children involved."

A simple monument honors the memory of the Roswell women.

After the Civil War ended, most of Roswell's wealthier families began returning to their formerly occupied city. The mills were rebuilt and reopened. Slavery became recognized as one of the great blemishes on the country and continued to cast its dark shadow for well over a century.

Pierce Mease Butler, unable to revive his inheritance without slave labor, died on the Georgia coast of malaria. Fanny Kemble supported herself by traveling across the United States and Europe performing Shakespearean readings until she died in

London. The book chronicling her winter on a Georgia plantation has remained in print for more than 150 years. Mittie Bulloch saw a son, and later a granddaughter, occupy the White House.

Surviving members of the Cherokee Nation were finally given land in North Carolina. The former plantation on Butler's Island became a state wildlife refuge, and the estate on St. Simons was forever erased by sprawl and development. Roswell King is buried in Founder's Cemetery; a large monument marks his legacy to the city that bears his name.

But the gravestones of the hundreds of displaced Roswell mill workers are scattered across the country, with few people knowing their whereabouts or what became of the women after they were taken from Roswell, Georgia, in the summer of 1864.

Chapter 18

a.k.a. Mayberry

OPIE: "The cage sure looks awful empty, don't it, Pa?"

ANDY: "Yes, son, it sure does . . . But don't the trees seem nice and full."

IT'S DIFFICULT TO RECALL THE PERIOD FROM 1960 TO 1968 IN AMERICA without also recalling the family gathered around the television set. Although the invention had been affordable for little more than a decade, by the sixties there was at least one TV in virtually every home in the country. An increasingly unpredictable world was suddenly brought into view as it had never been before—the Cuban Missile Crisis, the assassinations of the Kennedy brothers and Martin Luther King Jr., men walking on the moon. It was a time of such disparate political figures as Barry Goldwater, George Wallace, and Edmund Muskie. Americans were trying to make sense of changing values, free love and segregation, Vietnam and the Cold War.

The nightly news may have been delivered to our living rooms by such avuncular figures as David Brinkley and Walter Cronkite, but the woes of the planet were no less difficult to comprehend.

But during those first eight years of the tumultuous sixties, there was one brief escape from it all. For a sweet thirty minutes a week, by simply turning the dial, Americans could be nourished by the comfort food of television. There would be Andy and his barefooted son, Opie, walking down a dirt road to a fishing hole and to a slower rhythm of living than most people were experiencing. Just hearing that famous whistle from the theme song of *The Andy Griffith Show* makes at least two or three generations of Americans wistful for the softer times and good souls of Mayberry.

Mayberry-type cars still patrol. This is a classic patrol car in front of the Snappy Lunch diner.

It's all fiction, of course. Ever-steady, nurturing folks like Aunt Bee and Andy Taylor exist only in our dreams, and a real-life Mayberry is as rare as a two-headed rabbit. Right?

Maybe not.

If you make a beeline north of Charlotte, driving straight up Interstate 77 to the northwest corner of North Carolina, you'll come close to running into Mount Airy. When you park your car and start walking down Main Street, you may experience the sensation of returning to a place that is vaguely familiar and that might give you momentary calm if you've been chasing an elusive thing called home, or Mayberry.

And if you're like the thousands of other pilgrims who have made their way to this town in the foothills of the Blue Ridge Mountains, the first stop you'll probably make is at Floyd's City Barber Shop, the site that was voted the number one tourist attraction in town in the fall of 2004.

Once known as Mount Airy's City Barber Shop, it has been on the main drag in town for more than fifty years. Even with all the tourists, it's still possible to get a haircut here: "two chairs—no waiting" and the cost is "just seven dollars," according to the shop's owner, Russell Hiatt, "alias Floyd Lawson," who is eighty years old and still works five days a week.

"I'm the last barber here that ever cut Andy Griffith's hair," says Mr. Hiatt. "The barbershop is a prototype for Floyd's

Russell Hiatt, aka "Floyd the barber"

Barbershop on *The Andy Griffith Show*," he says, and on the walls of his shop are photographs of some of the countless tourists who have taken the road to Mayberry. "I've had 'em come from Japan, Africa, India, Switzerland, England, and from some little country outside of Russia that I can never remember. Every state and fourteen countries. I have almost 27,000 [photographs] right now, and I could have had five times that many."

Most of the tourists find Russell Hiatt's shop on their own and wander in, looking for the place where Andy and the other characters on the show passed time, gossiped, and occasionally shared a nugget of wisdom with one another. "And then we have bus tours," he says, especially during the tourist season when Mayberry Day is celebrated the last weekend in every September.

Andy Griffith, the town's undisputed most famous son, was born to Carl and

Mount Airy's most famous homeplace

Geneva Griffith in 1926, and the family lived on Haymore Street in Mount Airy. While for years the actor disclaimed any similarities between Mayberry and his hometown, the similarities are there.

"We used to have a deputy sheriff here, and it looked like he weighed about a hundred pounds," says Russell Hiatt. "Real tall and skinny. And when he'd get stuck making an arrest, he'd get so nervous, he had to have help. So, I think that's where Barney [played by Don Knotts] came from."

And Sheriff Taylor's Aunt Bee, the pillow-chested, flour-faced, sweet but no-nonsense elder relative who helped Andy raise Opie, was supposedly inspired by one of Griffith's real aunts, Grace Moore. The actress who portrayed Bee Taylor, the late Frances Bavier, retired to Siler City, a town that was often mentioned on the show. Among the real neighboring towns and people of Mount Airy, you'll find names that sound familiar to the show's fans: Pilot Mountain ("Mount Pilot"), Crumpler, North Carolina ("Helen Crump"), childhood friend Emmett Forrest and former town mayor E. T. Clark ("Emmett Clark"), the Beasleys ("Juanita" and "Goober"), Mulberry, North Carolina ("Mayberry"), and Taylorsville ("Andy Taylor").

Next door to Floyd's City Barber Shop is the Snappy Lunch, the oldest business in Mount Airy and a local eatery where, in one of the earliest episodes of the show, Andy suggested that Barney take a date "to eat, have some coffee, and talk." Charles Dowell, the owner of the Snappy Lunch, says that his hometown is not Mayberry. "But it is the closest that you will come to Mayberry. It's Mount Airy, but everything about it is what Mayberry portrayed on that show."

The series remained one of the top ten rated shows during its nearly decade-long run, and it was ranked number one when the show ended in April 1968. Most of it was filmed two thousand miles from North Carolina on a Desilu Studio's backlot in Culver City, California, where other successful shows of the period were filmed, including *Ozzie and Harriet, The Adventures of Superman, The Green Hornet, Lassie, Hogan's Heroes, Batman* and, later, some episodes of *Star Trek*. Yet in the 1960s and in nearly forty years of reruns that have followed, the majority of the show's viewers felt as if they were walking with Andy and Opie on the edge of a real-life Carolina lake and breathing real-life, pine-infused Carolina air. And they certainly felt as though the values and the people were real.

"Mount Airy is about as close as you'll get to Mayberry," says Alma Venable, who owns the Mayberry Motor Inn with her husband, Luther. "Mayberry is a state of mind. It's something that everyone would like to go back to. I have lived here [in Mount Airy] all my life. It is just a good place to live. A good place to be."

So much of what is seen today in Mount Airy is derived from *The Andy Griffith Show* that at first glance it is difficult to distinguish the "real" from the celluloid versions of people and landmarks. With more than seventy thousand tourists arriving annually, the name Mayberry now appears everywhere, from the Venables' motor inn (formerly called the Mount Airy Motor Inn), which has an Aunt Bee Room and is located on Andy Griffith Parkway, to the Mayberry Candle Shop, Mayberry Learning Center, and Mayberry Mall to Andy's Homeplace Bed & Breakfast and The Andy Griffith Playhouse.

Even Russell Hiatt, no man's fool and absolutely certain of himself, once told a reporter that "about 90 percent of people call me Floyd, and it got to the point I hardly recognized my own name."

Ann Vaughn, who works in the town's Visitors' Center says, "Of course, Andy

Griffith has stated that Mount Airy and Mayberry are two different entities—one being a fictional town, the other a real town—but be that as it may, we feel

Ann Vaughn: "We're like the mythical Mayberry."

that we were the inspiration for Mayberry and the people that come here really do think we're like the mythical Mayberry." And, she adds, "We do know that Andy and Don Knotts were major writers for the show, although they weren't listed [as writers in the credits]. So, they would definitely have to pull upon their background experiences to come up with those episodes on *The Andy Griffith Show*."

Although it's rare for Andy Griffith to return to Mount Airy—"he doesn't come here for a haircut," Russell Hiatt makes clear, and hasn't done so since he graduated from the University of North Carolina—he did come

home in the fall of 2004 for the unveiling of a statue of Andy and Opie and again later in the year for the funeral of the wife of his best friend in town.

"People love Andy Griffith," says Emmett Forrest, who is retired from the local electric company and has known the celebrity all his life. "They just don't like to see his shows and view him as an actor—they love Andy Griffith as a real live character.

"I have an Andy Griffith collection

Mayberry USA

here at the Visitors' Center," he continues. "I thought someone needed to pay tribute to Andy Griffith. And the only way that I knew I could help to pay that tribute was to accumulate and create this collection and offer it to the public to view. So, it's really my tribute to Andy Griffith."

"Mayberry is legendary because it is a part of most of our backgrounds," adds Ann Vaughn. "It is small town America. It's nostalgia. It's going back to the way it was. And I do feel that in today's society, as fast paced as it is, that we need to roll back those hands of time and look back to our roots." When asked what he thinks Mount Airy would be like today if there had never been *The Andy Griffith Show,* if there were no "Pink Floyd" T-shirts (with himself, the famous local and international barber all in pink) and no life-size Barney Fife posters and other Mayberry memorabilia for sale, Russell Hiatt thinks for a moment and then says, "I've been on this Main Street fifty-eight years. And I've seen it all," including the construction of a mall and a Walmart, "over on the highway in the fifties. But now we have Main Street with its shops and all this free publicity. I can't imagine what Mount Airy would be without Mayberry. Without it we would have been just about another ghost town."

And then he adds, "If you're loooking for the place on the map, it's not there. But in the hearts of people, it's here. People come here looking—looking for a quiet place, a simpler time, and all of that, and they go away happy.

"I try to do my part to keep it going."

Thank you, Floyd.

Chapter 19

Underground Wonders

THE LOST SEA AND RUBY FALLS REWARD ADVENTURERS BUT FRIGHTEN OTH-ERS. Are you brave enough to crawl into a dark cave and venture several hundred feet into the earth, not knowing what dangers—real and imagined—await you at the other end? That's precisely how two of the most dramatic natural wonders of the South were discovered.

The Lost Sea

In 1905, thirteen-year-old Ben Sands was exploring the land around his home in Sweetwater, Tennessee, located in the eastern part of the state about forty miles south of Knoxville and east of Chattanooga. The mountainous land had been home to the Cherokee Indians until President Andrew Jackson ordered their removal in 1838, so arrowheads, pottery, and other Native American artifacts were commonplace. But even more intriguing to a teenaged boy were the numerous caves created eons before by the violent upheavals that had formed the Appalachian Mountains. There are more than 3,800 known caves in Tennessee. A small, unobtrusive opening in the side of a hill may end within ten feet, or it may extend several hundred feet deep into a mountain before opening into a cavern. In fact, the network of caves in the Sweetwater area is called Craighead Caverns (in honor of a former Cherokee chieftain).

There is evidence that some of these caves existed more than twenty thousand years ago—early twentieth-century explorers found the skeletal remains of a giant Pleistocene jaguar that are now on display in the American Museum of Natural History in New York City. Prior to the arrival of the English settlers in the 1820s, the Cherokee used the caves for shelter, protection, and ceremonial functions. Settlers subsequently used them for storing potatoes and vegetables, since the constant temperature (about fifty-eight degrees) of the subterranean caves created natural refrigeration.

A generation later, Confederate Army troops mined the area caves for saltpeter—a white, gray, or colorless mineral of potassium nitrate used in making gunpowder—that

There are no waves on this underground sea.

had formed naturally over the years. And when Union armies overran the South late in the Civil War, the caves also provided temporary hiding places for the Confederates.

By the time young Ben Sands was exploring caves, most had been unused for years. He had no idea what to expect when he crawled through a thirty-six-inch opening and wriggled down a muddy cave that led nearly three hundred feet under ground. He passed through several large openings, connected by the narrow tunnel, before he finally reached a huge room filled with water. His meager lamp was no match for the thick darkness, so Sands threw mudballs as far as he could, trying to determine the size of the water-filled opening. He heard only splashes in every direction.

Legends about an underground lake predated the Cherokee, but no one had ever reported finding such . . . until Ben Sands climbed out of his cave. Soon others followed him to the site, and by 1915 local entrepreneurs had developed a plan for making the underground lake a tourist attraction. Difficult access through the original tunnel forced the creation of another entryway almost a mile away from the underground lake, so only the hale or immensely curious made the trek. And for most people, once was enough.

Within a few years, the Great Depression ended most travel and tourism, and moonshiners became the primary visitors to Craighead Caverns. The caves provided seclusion for their illegal stills and safe storage for their output. But the entrepreneurial spirit is hard to kill, and someone decided that anywhere there was liquor there ought to be dancing. Before you could say "Jimmy cracked corn," a dance floor was laid and the Cavern Tavern opened for business in the early 1940s. And before you could say ". . . and I don't care," it was closed. The cool, moist air inside the cavern apparently encouraged patrons to imbibe—often to excess. When those over-served patrons started to leave the Tavern, up a steep flight of 130 steps, they sometimes lost their balance and tumbled backwards, setting off a domino effect. A number of injuries persuaded the owners that alcohol and steep steps don't mix.

Guide Jamie Biondo keeps her flashlight close.

The next effort to monetize the caverns was a

commercial mushroom farm. Caves provided plenty of darkness and dampness for growing 'shrooms, but the transportation issues in and out of the mountains, especially in winter, overwhelmed the upside possibilities.

Finally in 1963, Ben Sands' cave was reopened as "The Lost Sea," a full-fledged tourist attraction. The cave walls were shored up, the entrance was widened, a ticket window/gift shop was built, and glass-bottom boats were added. Since that time, "The Lost Sea" has operated under private ownership and now includes a general store, ice cream parlor, trading post, and restaurant.

Its feckless past aside, "The Lost Sea" is truly a remarkable natural wonder. Located

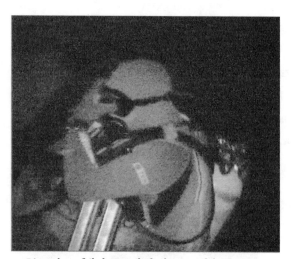

Divers have failed to reach the bottom of the Lost Sea.

three hundred feet under ground, it covers at least thirteen acres. The exposed surface is approximately eight hundred feet long and two hundred feet wide, but the bottom has never been reached. It is listed as the second largest underground lake in the world, just a couple acres smaller than one in Africa. Divers have tried several times to explore the depths of the cave, but bubbles from their breathing apparatuses dislodged chunks from the walls and discouraged further exploration.

In a 1970s attempt to discover if the lake emptied outside the cave, tagged trout were introduced into the water. The offspring of those aquatic trailblazers are still swimming in "The Lost Sea"—no signs of egress. Years of inbred evolution in a pitch-dark cave have left the fish mostly blind and far lighter in color than their cousins outside. Tour guides provide their only food, since nothing grows in the black water. The caves themselves, however, are alive with dramatic rock formations.

Stalactite and stalagmite formations are plentiful, creating the impression of an alien landscape under the artificial lighting. Many formations are colorfully named, such as the "Vale of Tears," "Crystal Falls," and "Betsy the Milking Cow." Still others are said to bear resemblance to George Washington or Abraham Lincoln . . . if you use your imagination. But most dramatic of all is

Colorful crystalline formations dot the landscape.

the presence of anthodites—clusters of radiating calcite or aragonite needles, sometimes called "cave flowers" or "orchids of the mineral kingdom." Geologists estimate that nearly 50 percent of the world's known anthodite formations are within Craighead Caverns. Consequently, "The Lost Sea" has been designated as a Registered National Landmark by the U.S. Department of the Interior.

If not for the curiosity of a thirteen-year-old boy, this natural wonder might still be "lost."

Ruby Falls

Serendipity led to another glorious underground discovery at nearby Lookout Mountain, just outside Chattanooga, Tennessee. Unlike Ben Sands' cave, Lookout Mountain Cave had been well known and explored for generations. Its location at the base of Lookout Mountain, just above the Tennessee River, had made it a favorite gathering place for Native Americans and later for visitors. One of the thousands of names written or etched on the walls of the cave is that of Andrew Jackson—the seventh president of the United States and a Tennessee resident at the time of his death in 1845. During the Civil War, the cave was used as a makeshift hospital for wounded troops, and many of the soldiers added their names and units to the autographs on the walls. One legend is that Confederate soldiers explored twelve miles into the cave without reaching the end.

A Manmade entrance provides easier access to cave.

In 1908, when the Southern Railway built a new line through the edge of Lookout Mountain, the entrance to the tunnel was permanently sealed. Leo Lambert, a local businessman and cave enthusiast, lamented the closing of the historic cave. So in 1923, he formed a corporation for the purpose of reopening Lookout Mountain Cave to the public. They purchased the land and in 1928 began blasting and drilling an elevator shaft that would afford new access to the old cave. They estimated the shaft would have to extend 420 feet straight down through solid limestone.

On December 28, 1928, a worker operating a jackhammer at a depth of approximately 260 feet hit a hollow spot. Lambert, called to investigate, felt a cool, moist draft of air that he recognized as the sign of a cave. He grabbed the barest of tools and set out to explore the opening, which measured only eighteen inches high and four feet wide. Several hours into his exploration, Lambert thought he heard running water and was lured on by the intriguing sound. Seventeen hours later after entering the small tunnel, Lambert returned with breathless tales of fantastic rock formations and a spectacular underground waterfall.

Few people believed that a waterfall could exist inside a mountain, so Lambert went back again and this time took his wife, Ruby, and several others. They corroborated his story and he named the newly discovered falls for his wife— Ruby Falls.

Work continued on the elevator shaft, and ninety-two days after digging had begun, they reached the old Lookout Mountain Cave. But now instead of one tourist attraction, Lambert's corporation had two. An impressive entrance building, modeled after a fifteenth-century

Surreal caves attract young and old to Ruby Falls.

Irish castle, was built from limestone excavated out of the mountain. The original historic cave was opened to the public on December 30, 1929, and the Ruby Falls cave opened June 16, 1930. From 1930-35, tours of both caves were offered and attracted many tourists. But Ruby Falls quickly became the overwhelming favorite, and the original cave was dropped from the tour.

What Leo Lambert saw on his first exploration, and what thousands of people have seen since, is the result of Nature at her most powerful and glorious. The series of earthquakes that likely formed the mountains lifted subterranean streams far above their original levels. The streams then dissolved the limestone layer of the earth and, over years and years, created caverns under the ground. The Lookout Mountain caverns are actually two caves—the original cave and the Ruby Falls cave directly above it. Both probably were formed at the same time. Minerals in the water, such

as calcium carbonate, dripped and seeped over time, creating fantastic formations on the cave's floor, ceiling, and walls. Some of the damp, white onyx stalagmites create the impression of being in an ice cave, while other stalactites may include multiple colors woven in rock. The largest formation at Ruby Falls, the Leaning Tower, is estimated to be between three and five million years old. Of course, without artificial lighting there would be no colors inside the pitch-black cave.

The impression is that of being in an ice cave.

The 145-foot waterfall that Lambert discovered—the highest in the United States open to the public—cascades into a crystal clear pool. At peak flow, an estimated three hundred gallons of water per minute go over the precipice, but unlike the contained "Lost Sea," water from Ruby Falls drains through the mountain and into the Tennessee River.

Leo Lambert was right about one thing, though: people come from all over the world to see his discovery—approximately four hundred thousand tourists per year. Mrs. Ruby Lambert must be very proud.

Chapter 20

Nuestra Señora de Atocha

"Once you have seen the ocean bottom paved
with gold, you never forget it!"

— *Mel Fisher*

LIKE MILLIONS OF YOUNG BOYS BEFORE HIM, MEL FISHER GREW UP READING Robert Louis Stevenson's *Treasure Island* and Herman Melville's *Moby Dick* and dreaming of a life of adventure on the high seas. Tales of exotic places and buried treasure were magical to an eleven-year-old in Glen Park, Indiana, where farming was the backdrop for most dreams.

But even at that early age, Mel Fisher's dreams didn't end at sunrise. He lived them every day. "There was a small lake down the street that Dad wanted to explore," said Kim Fisher, Mel's second-born son. "So he got an old paint bucket that would fit over his head, put a plastic window in the front and cut a hole for a hose. He attached the other end of the hose to a bicycle pump and had a friend pump air down to him so he could walk around in the lake and look for treasure. He almost drowned."

Fisher studied engineering at Purdue University and, with the outbreak of World War II, served with the U.S. Army Corps of Engineers. After the war he traveled a bit, including a stop in Florida where he was first exposed to diving and got his first glimpse of recovered treasure. His engineering bent also led him to experiment with making his own spear-guns, underwater cameras, and other diving equipment. In 1950, however, Fisher moved with his parents to Torrance, California, where they operated a chicken farm. "Dad said those chickens never took a day off," recalled son Kim.

About that time, French diver Jacques Cousteau invented the first SCUBA [self-contained underwater breathing apparatus] units that would revolutionize diving. "Dad bought the first five scuba tanks that were imported into the United States," said Kim. "He also bought a compressor to refill the tanks. He said in the next year he made more money selling air than eggs, so he sold the chicken farm."

In a twist that would strain the credibility of a romance novel, Fisher also got a life's mate in the deal. Dolores ("Deo") Horton, whose mother and uncle bought the chicken ranch, soon became Fisher's wife and diving companion. On their honeymoon, the couple went diving among shipwrecks in the Florida Keys. They returned with a plan to open the country's first "dive store," and they began diving commercially for spiny lobsters to fund the venture. In 1953 Mel and Deo opened Mel's Aqua Shop in Redondo Beach, California. By offering free diving lessons to anyone who bought equipment, they nurtured a recreational diving boom on the Left Coast.

Although there were fewer sunken treasure ships off the California coast than off the Florida coast, Fisher soon realized that there was plenty of submerged treasure in his geographic back yard. The riverbeds that had spawned the California Gold Rush of 1849 were virgin territory for a new breed of prospectors wearing scuba gear. More and more customers came to Mel's Aqua Shop . . . but most of them were men, which frustrated Deo. In an attempt to attract attention to their sport and show that women were every bit as capable as men, she decided to challenge the women's world record for staying underwater. On August 2, 1959, twenty-three-year-old Deo Fisher descended into an empty porpoise tank at the Hermosa Beach Aquarium—leaving her husband and three children, Dirk (five), Kim (three), and Kane (nine months) above ground. She surfaced fifty-five hours and thirty-seven minutes later with the new world's record.

Meanwhile, the Fishers continued going to Florida at every opportunity to dive and treasure hunt. The boy had become a man, but his childhood dreams remained.

On their way back from a diving expedition in 1964, the Fishers stopped in Sebastian, Florida, to meet Kip Wagner, a local treasure-hunter who operated an under-funded, underwater recovery business called Real Eight (a pun on eight reales, or "pieces of eight," referring to the Spanish milled silver dollars of the colonial period). Wagner's group had recovered

The irrepressible Mel Fisher

some coins from the 1715 Spanish Plate Fleet that had sunk off the coast between Sebastian and Fort Pierce, but the process had been slow and costly. Wagner offered the Fishers half interest in his operation, and they soon packed up the family and relocated, along with a group of experienced divers, to Florida. The Fishers' pursuit of sunken treasure became a formal business instead of a vacation pastime. The new company was called Universal Salvors (later renamed Treasure Salvors).

Diving around the coral reefs off the south Florida coast proved to be very difficult;

the same conditions that produced shipwrecks—rip tides and razor-like coral—also threatened divers. But the perseverance of the crew was finally rewarded with a major discovery. "They punched a hole in the sand and the ocean was carpeted with gold coins," said Pat Clyne, who joined Mel Fisher in 1972 after a stint as a shark hunter.

A recreation of a period masted ship

The find included thousands of gold coins, and the ensuing publicity led to a "gold rush" of treasure hunters to Florida. The State Legislature had to write new laws to govern the discovery and division of treasures recovered in the waters it controlled. Professional salvagers were required to enter into contracts with the state, get permits for salvaging, and turn over 25 percent of anything found. By 1968 Universal Salvors had recovered more than $20 million in treasure from the 1715 site and felt it was time to move on, so they relocated to the Keys where many more ships had wrecked.

"Mel had been reading all of the books and literature he could find on sunken ships," recalled Clyne. "One in particular was John Potter's *The Treasure Diver's Guide*. The book listed all the Spanish galleons that had sunk, and beside each name there were stars representing how much wealth was on the ship. Only one ship had four stars—the Nuestra Señora de Atocha. That was it. Mel was hooked."

Less than a century after Columbus bumped into the New World, Spain had colonized vast parts of Central and South America and was exploiting its riches and natural resources. Between 1561 and 1748, two fleets a year were sent from Cadiz, Spain, to the New World to transport supplies to the colonists and bring back gold, silver, and agricultural products for the home market. The fleets sailed *en masse* to the Caribbean, where half headed to Mexico and the other half to South America. Approximately two to three months later, they would reunite in the Caribbean and set sail for Spain. Each fleet usually had large galleons, fully staffed with warriors and weapons, at the front and back of the pack to protect against pirates or fleets from other countries.

The Nuestra Señora de Atocha was one such galleon that left Spain on March 23, 1622. It arrived at the port of Portobello, Panama, on May 24, where it was unloaded and then reloaded with treasures from Lima and Panama. It made another stop at Cartagena, Colombia, where it took on a large shipment of gold and silver from the recently established mint. The ship arrived in Havana, Cuba, in late August.

The Atocha, a relatively new ship, measured 110 feet long and carried 82 infantry-men and armaments, in addition to 183 others—crew and a large contingent of wealthy businessmen. Because it was considered especially safe, the Atocha was loaded with a disproportionate share of the riches (according to the official manifest, it was loaded with forty-seven tons of silver and gold). But no number of troops or cannons could protect the Spanish galleon from the fury of a hurricane.

On September 4, the fleet of twenty-eight ships set sail for Spain, and the Atocha took the rear-guard position. By the next morning, a fast-moving storm had churned into the region, creating huge waves. Strong winds pushed the front portion of the fleet into the calmer Gulf of Mexico, but five ships at the end of the line took the full brunt of the storm. Despite her weight, the Atocha was lifted high on a wave and smashed onto a coral reef. She sank instantly.

The next day a scant five survivors were found floating among the wreckage. The

Finding Spanish booty

hold of the Atocha sat on the bottom of the ocean, fifty-five feet below. Pearl divers, holding their breath, tried to begin salvage operations but could not break into the hatches. So the broken mast sticking out of the water was marked, and the crew returned to Havana for proper tools. Before they could return, however, a second storm battered the area. When they finally made it back, the Atocha's wreckage had vanished. Salvagers tried in vain for another decade to locate the sunken ship but to no avail. The financial loss staggered the Spanish rulers and hastened the decline of the empire.

The Atocha rested undisturbed in a watery grave for the next three and a half centuries.

Mel Fisher's Treasure Salvors had found seven wrecks since they started working the Florida waters, so he assumed that finding the Atocha would be no more challenging. In fact, the search for the Atocha would take far more time, money, and lives than anyone could have imagined.

Fisher began by researching the original wreck. He paid a Ph.D. student doing a thesis on the Atocha to decipher the original documents in the maritime museum in Seville, Spain. That research provided a general location, near the present-day Marquesas, about forty miles west of Key West. The Fishers moved their family to a houseboat in Key West to facilitate the process. For the next two years the team searched the ocean bottom with high-tech equipment, looking for any signs of metal. A couple of intriguing finds—a huge Spanish anchor and some olive jar fragments—lifted their spirits for a while, but then another two years passed without a significant find. Finally Mel's son Kane found a silver bar inscribed with numbers that matched those on the original Spanish manifest. This was the first real evidence that they were in the right place, but even this find was followed by another dry spell.

Through it all, Mel Fisher maintained his single-minded pursuit. He believed that every day would be "the day" when a single find or a clue would unlock the mystery of the Atocha's location.

On July 13, 1975, Mel's oldest son Dirk found five bronze cannons from the Atocha, and the team seemed certain that their efforts were about to be rewarded. But instead of riches, they encountered tragedy one week later. Dirk, his wife,

Divers search the seabed for lost treasure.

Angel, and diver Rick Cage all were lost over the salvage site when their boat capsized at night. "That was a devastating blow," said Kim Fisher. "That's the only time we ever thought about throwing in the towel, saying to heck with it. Dad sold off one of the boats. But then it was kind of a family decision that Dirk would want us to continue on. That decision actually increased our determination."

For the next ten years, the Atocha begrudgingly gave up tantalizing pieces of her treasure—gold coins, jewelry, and even pieces of wreckage—but the mother lode eluded searchers. Spirits rose and fell with each discovery. Frustration was matched only by increasing expenses. The State of Florida declared that it owned any treasure found in its waters, and the case (which lasted seven years and cost Fisher $1.6 million in legal fees) went to the U.S. Supreme Court before a "finders keepers" ruling was issued in Fisher's favor. (To avoid further litigation, Fisher reached a compromise with the State whereby he would donate twenty percent of any recovered artifacts to the State.) But through those difficult times, Mel Fisher never lost his focus or his positive attitude.

Fisher was the eternal optimist to his crew.

"Mel's motto was, 'Today's the day!'" said Pat Clyne. "We'd have a radio check three times a day, when he'd give us new information about where to look, where to dig, what to do. And he'd always end every conversation with, '. . . and today's the day!'" Fisher held parties for investors and speculators, always teasing their interest with the latest information on the search. He used the media to promote each new find. He did whatever it took to continue the search.

The task was made considerably easier by the 1980 discovery of millions of dollars in treasure from the Santa Margarita, one of the four ships lost along with the Atocha on that stormy September day in 1622. But as lucrative as that find proved to be, it was a consolation prize in Fisher's eyes. He wanted the Atocha.

On Memorial Day weekend of 1985, divers found a cache of thirteen gold bars, four pieces of emerald-studded gold jewelry, a gold chain, and coins. The trail was getting warmer. Six weeks later, on July 20, divers encountered a large reef that looked like stacked stones. As they investigated further, the stones turned out to be a wall of solid silver bars. Diver Andy Matroci broke the surface of the water yelling, "It's the mother lode! We're sitting on silver bars!"

Kane Fisher radioed back to Key West with the news: "Put away the charts. We've found the main pile!" Mel Fisher was out shopping for new diving fins when the call came, but friends tracked him down and shared the startling news. Sixteen years after the search had begun, almost ten years to the day after his son and daughter-in-law were lost at sea, and after spending approximately $10 million on his quest, Mel Fisher had found the treasure of Nuestra Señora de Atocha.

Eureka! Gold bars recovered from the wreck site

The recovered riches, pulled from the ocean's bed over the next couple of years, were estimated to be worth between $200 million and $400 million. They included nearly a thousand bars of silver weighing about seventy pounds each; boxes upon boxes of gold coins; more than 250 pounds of gold bars; more than three thousand Colombian emeralds; and hundreds of pieces of rare jewelry. It was the largest find of lost treasure since the 1930s discovery of King Tut's tomb.

The archeological value of the Atocha's discovery is every bit as rich as its gold, silver, and gems. In 1973, Fisher had the foresight to hire an archeologist as a member of his crew to ensure that no damage was done to historic sites during his searches for treasure. Extensive documentation was done on each search site. Many of the relics themselves went on display for the world to see. With part of his share of treasure from the Atocha, Fisher bought a former Key West naval station and started the non-profit Mel Fisher Maritime Heritage Society Museum, where some of the treasure and related research is housed. There's also a Mel Fisher Center in Sebastian, Florida, that exhibits finds from other Fisher expeditions. Fisher's family still manages the business and continues searching for sunken artifacts.

Mel Fisher died of cancer in December 1998, but not before he realized the dreams that had filled the imagination of an eleven-year-old boy in Indiana so many years ago.

Chapter 21

See Rock City!

"I think my sign for Rock City is more famous than Rock City."
— *Clark Byers*

SINCE THE EARLY 1920s, WHEN AMERICA FIRST BECAME A NATION OF CONSUMERS and a nascent advertising industry sprang up in midtown New York, the term *Madison Avenue* has been synonymous with upscale advertising. During the past eighty years, catchy taglines such as "See the USA in a Chevrolet," fictional pitchmen and women like The Jolly Green Giant and Betty Crocker, and memorable phrases like "*plop plop, fizz fizz*" have produced millions of dollars in sales.

But it's doubtful that any Madison Avenue firm ever conceived a more cost-effective and successful ad campaign than the one Garnet Carter devised in 1932 to promote his wife's garden:

SEE ROCK CITY!

Carter had grown up on Lookout Mountain, a craggy peak on the Georgia-Tennessee border just outside Chattanooga. The mountain had been a popular spot for more than a century, first with Native Americans and later with settlers. In 1823, missionary Daniel Butrick wrote in his diary about "a citadel of rocks" on Lookout Mountain where huge boulders were positioned in such a way "as to afford streets and lanes."

By the time of the Civil War, the mountaintop was already being called "the Rock City," and people marveled at how far they could see on a clear day. Lookout Mountain remained a popular spot for hikers into the twentieth century.

As a young man, Garnet Carter became a natural promoter and dabbled in a number of businesses. One of his ventures in the early 1920s was trying to develop a high-end, residential community atop Lookout Mountain. The new community—to be called Fairyland because of his wife, Frieda's, fascination with the fairies of European folklore—was supposed to include a golf course to capitalize on the sport's booming growth. But building a golf course was more complicated and took longer than Carter imagined, and his new residents were getting restless.

In classic entrepreneurial fashion, Carter solved his problem by building what is now considered to be the first miniature golf course in America. His Tom Thumb golf facility (a name in keeping with Frieda's fairy fetish) opened in 1927 and was immediately so successful that Carter franchised the concept throughout the U.S.

While Garnet was launching a miniature golf industry, Frieda was literally sowing the seeds of another industry. Using twine to mark the trail, she laid out paths through ten acres of mammoth rock formations, ending at a dramatic overlook called Lover's Leap. She then planted more than four hundred varieties of wildflowers and other indigenous vegetation beside the trails to create a dramatic rock garden. Statues of gnomes and fairies, most imported from Europe, stood sentry all along the 4,100-foot trail.

Garnet Carter, always listening for opportunity's knock, soon realized that people might pay to enjoy his wife's mountaintop garden and the dramatic views from overlooks. So on May 21, 1932, Rock City Garden officially opened as a tourist attraction.

With the country three years into the Great Depression, business was understandably slow. Even so, thousands of people were passing through nearby Chattanooga every week on U.S. Highway 41, most of them headed south as part of the great Florida land boom.

Highway 41—opened in the late 1920s—was a major north-south corridor, stretching nearly two thousand miles through eight states, from Copper Harbor, Michigan, to Naples, Florida. If Carter could find a way to entice motorists to leave the highway and stop off at Rock City Garden, he knew the attraction would be successful. Carter enlisted the brainstorming help of friend and fellow promoter Fred Maxwell. What they needed was a very big sign to alert passing motorists. As they drove around the area, they spotted the palettes for such signs—the sides of a thousand barns that lined Highway 41.

Block Brothers Tobacco Company of Wheeling, West Virginia, had conceived a similar plan back before the turn of the century. It started painting "Chew Mail Pouch Tobacco" on the sides of barns as early as 1897 and continued the practice until 1993. More than twenty thousand barns from Pennsylvania through the Midwest, and all the way to the Pacific Northwest, advertised Mail Pouch chewing tobacco at one time or another.

Carter decided to try the same approach. Late in 1935, he hired a twenty-two-year-old apprentice sign painter who worked for his friend Maxwell. "I was just a kid working as a sign painter's helper. Mr. Maxwell took me up on Lookout Mountain to meet Mr. Carter, and that's how it all started," remembered Clark Byers years later.

In the beginning, Carter and Maxwell would drive up and down the highway selecting potential sign barns. Then Byers, in an old truck loaded with paint and ladders, would be sent out to strike a deal. "I was so bashful and backwards in them days, I'd walk up to a house just hoping nobody was home."

Clark Byers with the tools of his trade

The opening offer usually would be "a free coat of paint on your barn or roof," but when farmers realized the paint job was actually an advertisement, they sometimes wanted a little more. "I'd take along free passes, Rock City bathmats or thermometers and offer them, and if that didn't work, I'd pay 'em anywheres from $3 to $5 for the use of their barns," said Byers. "Back then, $3 would buy maybe two sacks of flour or something like that. We'd redo the signs ever' two years.

"I'll never forget one day I started painting a roof, and the man didn't understand that it was gonna be a sign. He come home later, and when he saw the sign, he said, 'Looks like a dog's rear tied up with hickory bark.' But he let me keep it up there."

The paint scheme was as simple (and inexpensive) as it was effective—white type on a solid black background. "I mixed up my own paint using lampblack and linseed oil," recalled Byers. "First thing I did was black out the roof. There was no such thing as rollers back then—I used a four-inch brush. Once that paint got on, there was no getting it off. Then I'd take a piece of white chalk and hit the tops of the nail heads where I wanted the letters. Painted all the letters freehand. Never even measured."

The original message was equally simple—"See Rock City." The word *garden* was omitted to save time and space. As the signs spread across the countryside, the messages became more varied:

> Stay on U.S. 41 and See Rock City!
> See 7 States From Rock City!
> When You See Rock City, You See the Best!
> To Miss Rock City Would Be a Pity!

Byers also tired of following directions to barns selected by Carter and Maxwell. "There was an ol' roof down at Tunnel Hill, Georgia, about seventy-five feet long," Byers said in a *Fiddlers Green* story. "They [Carter and Maxwell] hadn't ever seen it. They'd been by there, but it was settin' in behind some trees. I knew if I could cut the trees down it would knock their eyes out, so I got permission to cut the trees and paint that barn. You could see it at least three-quarters of a mile—that's how good it was. It was so much better than anything they had ever picked out, and they didn't even know it was there. So from then on, they just turned me loose and let me pick the sites."

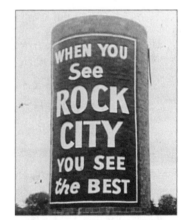

Any surface was a suitable palette.

Byers added a couple of assistants, and "on a good day we could do three or sometimes four barns. We didn't miss a lick. We was hungry and in a hurry," he recalled. Although tin roofs could get extremely hot during summer months, those were peak production times: "The paint works real good when the weather's hot." They also traveled farther and farther from home, painting signs

Byers lived to see his work become historic sites.

along the northern reaches of Highway 41. "I would dread goin' out on the road so bad till I got about fifty miles away from home. Once I got about fifty miles, it was all over then. I'd work my head off to get back home. One time we were up on the Tennessee-Kentucky line and I wrote Mr. Carter a postcard: 'Out of paint and out of money. Going home to see my honey.'"

After several hundred signs, Byers did unusual things to break the monotony. He started painting signs backward to attract more attention. "But one time I got down after painting a roof and saw I'd spelled *city* C-T-I-Y. That pretty much broke me of backwards painting," said Byers.

Attendance at Rock City seemed to grow in direct proportion to the highway signs. By the early 1950s, tens of thousands of people each year visited Frieda Carter's garden atop Lookout Mountain. In an attempt to provide something new to sell to tourists, Byers made miniature red barns and painted their roofs in the familiar black and white "See Rock City" scheme. He intended them to be used as mailboxes, but the Postal Service objected, saying they weren't regulation mailboxes. So, much to the joy of bluebirds everywhere, Byers cut holes in the sides of the boxes and made them into birdhouses. The distinctive birdhouses have been best-sellers at Rock City for more than half a century.

Garnet Carter, always the promoter, knew that adults were more likely to visit Rock City if there was something fun for the kids to do. So in the early 1950s he and Frieda created Fairyland Caverns by carving large holes into the rocks, providing natural stages for fairytale characters to act out their stories. Another winner. By 1960 Rock City was so popular that *Life* magazine featured it on the cover.

Garnet Carter died in 1954, and Frieda died a decade later (1964). Ownership of the attraction remained in the family, and through it all Clark Byers continued painting and repainting signs.

By 1968, Byers had painted nearly nine hundred "See Rock City" signs across nineteen states. Thirty-three years was a long time to be climbing barns and painting roofs. The interstate highway system had taken many people off the old thoroughfares like Highway 41, and the road-side sign industry was also under attack from the government and former First Lady Lady Bird Johnson. The Highway Beautification Act of 1966—also called the "Lady Bird Law"—placed extreme limitations on such painted advertisements.

"That Lady Bird Johnson was a trouble-maker," said Byers. "She wanted to do away with the old barns. I'll tell you what I call beauty: riding down across the country, and you got a bunch of old rusty barn tops. Then a while later

Some of the historic signs are still maintained today.

you come back through and you got a bunch of black and white *SEE ROCK CITY* on top of 'em covering up all that crap. Now, that's what I call beauty."

Age and new regulations may have led Clark Byers to consider retirement, but it took a powerful shock in 1969 to seal the deal. "I was working on a roof outside Murfreesboro, Tennessee," he recalled. "I don't know if it was lightnin' or a live wire hitting the roof, but it sounded like a dynamite blast right at my head. They said I was hit with 7,200 volts . . . enough to kill a dozen mules. It burnt some of the hair off my head." The electrical shock left Byers temporarily paralyzed and permanently retired as a sign painter. He subsequently owned and operated Sequoyah Caverns, a tourist attraction and campground in north Alabama, only thirty-seven miles from Rock City.

Fewer than one hundred of the barns Byers painted remain standing today, and most of those are still maintained by Rock City. A 1997 book of photographs by David B. Jenkins, *Rock City Barns: A Passing Era*, also serves to keep the artwork alive. Three states—Tennessee, Ohio, and West Virginia—have declared the barns historic sites.

Clark Byers died on February 19, 2004, at age eighty-nine.

Rock City remains a major tourist attraction. The facility, managed by Frieda and Garnet Carter's great-nephew, Bill Chapin, draws more than a half-million visitors each year. And the simple, three-word sales pitch that Clark Byers painted on barns—**SEE ROCK CITY**—has been etched in the history of the South.

Chapter 22

The Greenbrier's Secret

DON DELILLO, THE ENIGMATIC AMERICAN NOVELIST, ONCE SAID, "MEN WITH secrets tend to be drawn to each other, not because they want to share what they know but because they need the company of the like-minded, the fellow afflicted." Maybe that explains how the small town of White Sulphur Springs, West Virginia, was able to keep a classified secret from the rest of the world for thirty years.

Located at the base of the Allegheny mountain range on the Virginia–West Virginia border, White Sulphur Springs has been a tourist attraction for more than two centuries. Its cool summer temperatures, fresh air, and beautiful vistas—all because of its two-thousand-foot elevation above sea level—are allure enough, but they aren't the main draw. A natural spring, with high sulfate content and a constant temperature of 62.5 degrees Fahrenheit, has attracted visitors since 1778.

The water from the spring was thought to have curative powers, and many people endured difficult traveling conditions to reach the remote site where they could "take the waters." By the 1830s, thanks to a stagecoach route, White Sulphur Springs became a summer residence for many prominent planters, lawyers, merchants, and their families, who built clusters of cottages. And by 1858, the village had gained such a heady reputation that a three-story hotel—officially named the Grand Central Hotel, but called The Old White Hotel by regulars—was opened. During the Civil War, both sides occupied the site at different times and used its facilities as a hospital and a headquarters. But immediately after the war, the village returned to its *raison d'être*. The Chesapeake and Ohio Railway built a line right through town, and from that point on White Sulphur Springs was a widely popular resort. Guests came from as far away as Chicago, New York, and Atlanta.

In 1910, the Chesapeake and Ohio Railway decided to extend its investment and bought seven thousand acres, the resort cottages, and the old hotel for $150,000. A major renovation and expansion were begun, and in 1913 the new Greenbrier Hotel opened for business. The plush facility included a pool and an eighteen-hole golf course, designed by the famed Scotsman, Charles Blair Macdonald. A year later the hotel opened for year-round business. Among its guests during that inaugural year were President and Mrs. Woodrow Wilson and Joseph and Rose Kennedy, who traveled from Boston for their October honeymoon. The Greenbrier's growing popularity led to another expansion a decade later, when the Old White Hotel was leveled.

The White Sulphur Springs property played an interesting role in World War II, just as it had during the Civil War. Following the attack on Pearl Harbor in December 1941, and America's subsequent entry into the war, the U.S. State Department leased the Greenbrier for seven months and interned German, Japanese, and Italian diplomatic personnel and their families there until they could be exchanged for stranded American diplomats. When that lease expired, the U.S. Army purchased the Greenbrier and recast it as a two-thousand-bed hospital called Ashford General

Hospital. More than twenty-four thousand soldiers were treated at the facility before the end of the war in June 1945.

The Chesapeake and Ohio Railway reacquired the property from the government in 1946 and remodeled it for hotel and spa purposes. During the next several decades, the Greenbrier became one of the world's most respected resorts, offering fine lodging, dining, spa, and golf. But while the public face of the Greenbrier was widely displayed in travel magazines, newspapers, and on television, something very private was transpiring behind a curtain of secrecy.

Almost immediately after the end of World War II, tensions mounted between the Soviet Union and its allies, often referred to as the Eastern Bloc, and the United States and its allies, called the Western Bloc. The Soviets, under the leadership of Joseph Stalin, accused the U.S. of imperialism and trying to install capitalistic governments around the world. The U.S. charged that the Soviets were trying to spread communism and had erected an "iron curtain" across Eastern Europe.

The grandiose Greenbrier, nestled among the trees

As the two sides dug in with their competing ideologies, tension rose worldwide. That constant state of suspicion and mistrust—just short of actual fighting—came to be called the "Cold War," so named by presidential adviser Bernard Baruch. Since both the Soviets and the U.S. had atomic bombs at their disposal, it was generally feared that the next world war could be devastating beyond imagination and even threaten the survival of either culture.

Amid such fears, the U.S. government began making contingency plans. They needed a safe place for the president and the Congress —preferably apart—during an attack, and a place where they could be sustained afterward while governing a stricken nation. This safe place needed to be close enough to Washington, D.C., to afford speedy travel, yet far enough away to survive an attack on the seat of government. It needed to be somewhat isolated, so that preparations could be made in private, yet have sophisticated communications and support operations. Most important of all, its location needed to be secret so that the Soviets wouldn't target the safe haven with another missile.

Two hundred miles south of Washington, D.C., was a site that satisfied many of those requirements. Isolated but accessible, sophisticated support systems in place, and a small population that could keep a secret, the Greenbrier—where the U.S. Army had operated a hospital only a few years before—was ideal.

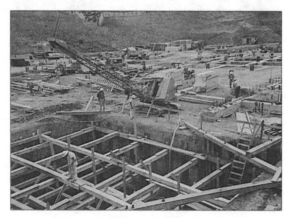

Construction of the new wing took four years.

In 1958, The Greenbrier was scheduled to begin another major expansion. This time an entire new wing would be added to the hotel. In exchange for government financing of the new wing, the hotel agreed to allow the simultaneous construction of an underground bunker, designed to be an emergency relocation center that would sustain the entire U.S. Congress in the event of war. The Greenbrier construction would provide excellent cover for the government project, originally called "Project Casper" but ultimately named "Project Greek Island." Approximately $14 million was allocated for the facility during President

Dwight D. Eisenhower's administration.

Secure tunnels led deep into the mountain.

The first clue to local contractors that there was something unusual about this building was the extraordinary amount of concrete being used. The walls of the underground portion of the facility are two feet thick and reinforced with steel. The hotel explained that it was simply building a lower-level exhibit hall that could double as a fallout shelter, just as many individuals were building bomb shelters in their basements. But the ceiling was also two feet thick, and it was covered with twenty feet of dirt. Over the next three years, the underground structure and the bristling new West Virginia wing of the Greenbrier were completed. Ironically, the facility became operational just weeks before the Cuban missile crisis in October 1962.

The outside entrance to the bunker was hidden behind aluminum doors with a sign warning *Danger: High Voltage,* just like any backup generator for a large facility would be marked. Inside an anteroom are two huge doors—each approximately fifteen feet high, twelve feet wide, twenty inches thick, and together weighing more than twenty-five tons. The hinges alone are said to weigh one and a half tons each, and yet the balance of the doors is so precise that a mere fifty pounds of force will

An unimposing door hid an imposing secret.

open or close them. With locks activated, the doors were designed to withstand a nuclear blast.

The bunker had its own power generating system, backup generators that could operate for forty to forty-five days on diesel fuel stored on the premises, a separate water system, and an elaborate filtration system that assured safe, fresh air or recycled air for the 112,000-square-foot complex. State-of-the-art communications systems were continuously updated and tested.

Congress would have slept in dormitory-like rooms.

Food supplies—enough to feed a thousand people for sixty days—were kept fresh, as were medical supplies for the hospital complex, which included an ICU and operating room. Other areas in the underground labyrinth included a decontamination room, an incinerator that could double as a crematorium, dormitories, a dining room that could seat four hundred, lounge space, bathrooms, and separate meeting rooms for the House of Representatives and the Senate.

For several years local speculation continued about the huge underground building in the town of approximately two thousand residents. But since there weren't a lot of "government types" moving into the area, the rumors settled quietly into passivity. Also, the Greenbrier provided more than 90 percent of the jobs available to the local workforce, and as every dog knows, you don't bite the hand that feeds you.

So where were the government types needed to manage and maintain such a facility, one that had to be fully operational with only four to eight hours notice? A cover company, Forsythe Associates, was created.

Forsythe Associates "functioned as a concessionaire to the hotel, providing audio/video support to the hotel," Paul Fritz Bugas, on-site superintendent of the Greenbrier bunker for more than two decades, explained in a PBS interview:

> We spent about 15 or 20 percent of our time doing A/V work for the hotel—repairing TVs—and about 80 percent of our time doing all the necessary work in the government facility. . . . There were about twelve to fifteen government employees on-site on a permanent basis. We wore a pair of slacks and a shirt to work just like all the other hotel employees, so everybody accepted us. . . . We melded into the community. We lived in the various little villages in an around the Greenbrier.

Robert Conte, official historian of the Greenbrier, said: "Every now and then I would meet somebody who seemed to know something about this, and I would back off. There was something very scary about this whole thing. I thought, *This is a serious secret, and I'm not supposed to know*."

So for thirty years, as guests came and went from the highly rated Greenbrier resort, and as the Watergate break-in and a thousand other secrets were uncovered by the national media, the government maintained a doomsday readiness facility in the hills of West Virginia without anyone noticing. That is, not until 1992.

"One of the scariest moments of my life was when this reporter [Ted Gup of the *Washington Post*] walked into my office, put a tape recorder on my desk and said, 'I'm here to talk about what's under the West Virginia wing,'" recalled Conte. "I looked at him, gulped, and said, 'Why, there's nothing under the West Virginia wing,' and I gave him the story of how it was built, but it was obvious he didn't believe a word I said."

The *Post* article ran on May 31, 1992, under the headline, "The Ultimate Congressional Hideaway," and it exposed the history of the bunker to the entire world. Sensitive material was removed from the bunker and relocated within twenty-four hours.

"I was devastated when the *Post* article ran," said Bugas, the facility's superintendent at the time, in his PBS interview. "We all felt a disservice had been done. I'm not talking to us personally, but to our country's security."

Even many local residents were stunned by the full revelations. "All the years I knew Fritz [Bugas], he never let on," said Dick Brockway, a retired forester who had lived in the area for decades. "There'd been local rumors that the Greenbrier was hiding something significant, but not in a million years would I have guessed that Fritz was involved in it."

Conte agreed: "What astonished me was not so much that it was here, but the extent of the program and the audacious nature of the plan—bringing the entire Congress down here. In other words, the reality was way beyond the rumors."

Once the secret was exposed and the facility compromised, the incredible underground complex was decommissioned by the government and became a tourist attraction in its own right. One former employee of Forsythe Associates became a tour guide, leading groups on a ninety-minute walk through the bunker.

Historian Robert Conte summed up the ultimate irony of the Greenbrier bunker: "A lot of people have looked up to the Greenbrier over the years as the height of civilization, so it was pretty startling to find out that something right here was designed for the end of civilization."

Index

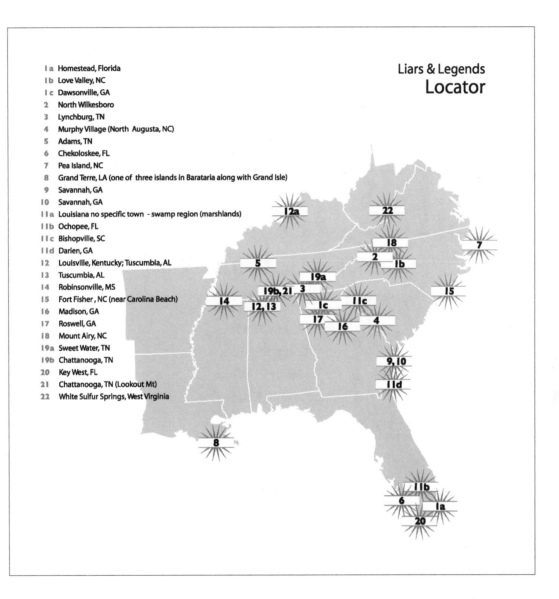

Liars & Legends
Locator

1 a   Homestead, Florida
1 b   Love Valley, NC
1 c   Dawsonville, GA
2   North Wilkesboro
3   Lynchburg, TN
4   Murphy Village (North Augusta, NC)
5   Adams, TN
6   Chekoloskee, FL
7   Pea Island, NC
8   Grand Terre, LA (one of three islands in Barataria along with Grand Isle)
9   Savannah, GA
10   Savannah, GA
1 1 a   Louisiana no specific town - swamp region (marshlands)
1 1 b   Ochopee, FL
1 1 c   Bishopville, SC
1 1 d   Darien, GA
12   Louisville, Kentucky; Tuscumbia, AL
13   Tuscumbia, AL
14   Robinsonville, MS
15   Fort Fisher , NC (near Carolina Beach)
16   Madison, GA
17   Roswell, GA
18   Mount Airy, NC
19a   Sweet Water, TN
19b   Chattanooga, TN
20   Key West, FL
21   Chattanooga, TN (Lookout Mt)
22   White Sulfur Springs, West Virginia

Acknowledgments

Additional research provided by

Jennifer Wysocki

Bryan Simmons

Corey Stienecker

Michael White

Teague Kennedy

Illustrations by

Karen Gold

John Roche